SACRED STONE

DEDICATED TO

MY HUSBAND, JEFFREY SWINTON, AND
LEE'S WIFE, JEANINE GROBERG

Cover design copyrighted 2002 by Covenant Communications, Inc.

Published by Covenant Communications, Inc.
American Fork, Utah

Printed in Canada
First Printing: May 2002

09 08 07 06 05 04 03 02   10 9 8 7 6 5 4 3

ISBN 1-59156-031-4

SACRED STONE

The Temple at Nauvoo

HEIDI S. SWINTON

Author of the documentary film by Lee Groberg

ACKNOWLEDGEMENTS

The Nauvoo Temple is more than a building; it is the beginning point of a journey for thousands of Latter-day Saints in the nineteenth century. And millions today. I wrote both the book and the companion documentary in tandem using journals and recollections of early Nauvoo residents, newspaper accounts of the time, interviews with noted scholars conducted by Lee Groberg specifically for this project, and frequent visits to Nauvoo to witness and chronicle the effort to rebuild this singular structure.

Further elaboration of *Sacred Stone* is found in the host of pictures taken by Lee as he did double duty directing the filming of the documentary and capturing images for the book as well. The contemporary images add so much, as do the many historical photographs and artifacts provided by The Church of Jesus Christ of Latter-day Saints and other archives.

Lee and I both express gratitude to Covenant Communications—Lew Kofford, Shauna Nelson, Margaret Weber, and Jessica Warner, whose vision, support, and uncompromising skill gave life to these pages. The KBYU sponsorship of the documentary made the whole project possible.

We are also grateful to the Temple Department and its Nauvoo representatives for their willingness to help us shape this story; to Legacy Constructors Rich Holbrook and Gael Maer for their patience in answering questions and allowing us to tag along on site; and to all the laborers and contractors who applied the same determination and devotion to the temple as did the early builders. I could read of this exceptional experience in their eyes as well as in the work of their hands. Thank you.

To all the historians, archivists, writers, and researchers who for years have studied and shaped our understanding of the Nauvoo Temple; to the noted scholars and experts who have expressed their impressions of the temple in this volume, thank you for your insights, discoveries, and excellent efforts.

Most of all, I honor my husband Jeffrey for his great strength, his support and encouragement, his faith in me, his thoughtful critiques, his championing of my efforts. And to our children, great appreciation for standing beside me—Cameron and Kristen, Daniel and Julia, Jonathan, and our Temple laborer Ian whose summer work in Nauvoo gave me insight I could not have gained without him.

Heidi S. Swinton
Salt Lake City, Utah

CONTENTS

Preface

o other story in American religious history can match the drama of the Mormon effort to build the kingdom of God on earth—a temple at its center. The near completion of the Nauvoo Temple in 1845 and the Saints' experiences within its walls represented "the beginning of a new era. . . . the beginning of a homeward journey."[1]

The story of the Nauvoo Temple is so much more than the account of constructing a building, its limestone walls, and distinctive carved stones of the sun, moon, and stars. It is about a people and their commitment to God, their willingness to gather together, leave homes and families, face rancor and persecution, poverty, sickness, disappointment, and even death to fulfill what was to them a divine command. Their effort was shaped not day-to-day, but with an eye to "eternal glory." Their hope was to build a house suitable for God, a house where they could be taught and blessed by promises of salvation. Most had little idea what that really meant, but they labored faithfully, nevertheless.

Their use of the temple for special religious rites was epoch in importance, but only weeks as we measure time. Yet it was enough time for nearly 6,000 to receive all they had hoped at the hands of the Lord's anointed. "December 20, 1845. Saturday . . . 564 Persons have passed

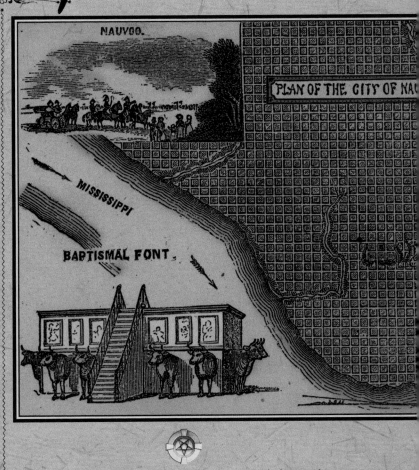

Above: The original plan for Nauvoo included a grid street pattern, farms outside the town, and a prominent location for a temple. It served as a model for later Mormon settlements.

Opposite: More than half the homes in the city were log structures with mud-chinked walls. The mortar was made of clay mixed with horsehair.

The real story of Nauvoo is the story of building a temple.

through, 95 this day," wrote William Clayton in the official record of the Nauvoo Temple.[2] "Passed through" seems an odd term for the culmination of a work that took an entire community five years of sacrifice and grueling labor. Yet the term fits so well when we understand that to these LDS faithful—as it had been to the ancients—"passing through" the temple was synonymous with opening "the gate of heaven."

Said Sarah Rich of that singular time, "Many were the blessings we had received in the House of the Lord, which has caused joy and comfort in the midst of all our sorrows, and enabled us to have faith in God, knowing He would guide us and sustain us in the unknown journey that lay before us."[3] For them, the journey ahead was much more than the forced exodus west; the journey was going home to God.

In the temple hung maps illustrating the wilderness to be settled—part of the journey that lay ahead of them. But the rites of the temple were so much more significant than the decor. They, too, were directions for a journey so sacred that Apostle George A. Smith admonished the Saints, "whatever transpires here ought not to be mentioned any where else."[4] The solemnity of the temple experience for the LDS faithful has not changed.

Hence, the writing of this account of the building and rebuilding of the Nauvoo Temple focuses on how they did it and why, without compromising the essence of the experience inside. Suffice it to say that participants shared the feelings of Joseph Kingsbury who wrote, "these blessings I feel to be thankful for and I pray I may always remember the goodness of the Lord to me."[5]

This book joins with the television documentary *Sacred Stone: Temple on the Mississippi*, produced by Lee B. Groberg, to tell the remark-able story of the Nauvoo Temple. But the essence of the story is not size, dimensions, timetables, and floor plans. Nor is it the story of the town. For years, the Latter-day Saints have told of Nauvoo, elaborating on its picturesque setting, the social, cultural, and economic development of a boomtown on the river. Somewhere in the chronicle, the temple is given a chapter. Then the commentary returns to the brick buildings on the flat, and the accounts of growth and business. Curious. For the real story of Nauvoo is the story of building a temple. Saints gathered to Nauvoo by divine command to build the temple. The economic structure of the town embraced the practice of tithing one day in ten to temple labor. The visitors who streamed into town came to view the enormous public works project on the hill. Children ran about the walls until they reached a height that was dangerous; patrols guarded the facility at night; distant congregations as far away as England contributed to the building coffers. And all who were engaged in the work of the temple were promised entrance when it was finished. Nauvoo was a Mormon town; and the centerpiece of Mormon worship—as taught by Prophet Joseph Smith and then elaborated by President Brigham Young—was clearly the temple. They called it "a house of prayer . . . a house of order, a house of God" (D&C 109:8).

The Saints who built this temple were seeking God's presence on the fringes of the frontier. They asked for peace; they did not get it in calm or tranquility. But they received in the temple the jump-start for their wilderness journey—the privilege of joining God through ordinances received in His holy house. On the wall of the temple they left a message in brilliant gold letters: "Come After Us."

Opposite: Detail of a sunstone showing a hand holding a trumpet. The number of "hands" working on the temple steadily increased, with the greatest progress being made on the structure in 1845 as it neared completion.

Below: This earliest-known sketch of the Nauvoo Temple by William Weeks, 1842, shows many of the significant features incorporated in the final design, including the elliptical arched window in the attic story.

INTRODUCTION

The town lay as in a dream, under some deadening spell of loneliness from which I almost feared to wake it; for plainly it had not slept long. There was no grass growing up in the paved ways; rains had not entirely washed away the prints of dusty footsteps.

I went about unchecked . . . into empty workshops, ropewalks and smithies. . . . No one called out to me from any opened window, or dog sprang forward to bark an alarm.

I could have supposed the people hidden in the houses, but the doors were unfastened; . . . I found dead ashes white upon the hearths. . . . On the outskirts of town was the city graveyard; but there was no record of plague.

Fields upon fields of heavy-headed yellow grain lay rotting ungathered upon the ground. No one was there to take in their rich harvest.

Col. Thomas L. Kane

On the southern suburb, the houses looking out upon the country showed, by their splintered wood-work and walls battered to the foundation, that they had lately been the mark of a destructive cannonade. And in and around the splendid Temple, which had been the chief object of my admiration, armed men were barracked, surrounded by their stacks of musketry and pieces of heavy ordnance.

MANSION HOUSE

They told the story of the Dead City; that it had been a notable manufacturing and commercial mart, sheltering over twenty thousand persons; that they had waged war with its inhabitants for several years, and had been finally successful only a few days before my visit.

They also conducted me inside the massive sculptured walls of the curious Temple, in which they said the banished inhabitants were accustomed to celebrate the mystic rites of an unhallowed worship. They particularly pointed out to me certain features of the building which . . . they had, as a matter of duty, sedulously defiled and defaced.

The city—it was Nauvoo, Illinois. The Mormons were the owners of that city, and the smiling country around. And those who had stopped their ploughs, who had silenced their hammers, their axes, their shuttles, and their workshop wheels; those who had put out their fires, who had eaten their food, spoiled their orchards, and trampled under foot their thousands of acres of unharvested bread; these were the keepers of their dwellings, the carousers in their Temple.

—Colonel Thomas L. Kane, September 1846

The story of the Nauvoo Temple is, for most people, but a footnote in America's nineteenth-century march to the Pacific. To the Latter-day Saints, the building of the Nauvoo Temple is a benchmark chapter in the history of this religion raised on American soil. The temple took five years to complete, yet was used by the faithful for only six weeks. It is a curious saga.

Why build a temple? Was not a church or meetinghouse sufficient for communion with God? These faithful followers of Christ believed as did those in ancient times that temples are houses of God where the Lord can reveal to His people the glories of His kingdom and the special ordinances and spiritual covenants necessary for their salvation. It was in the temple that time and space came together, where barriers collapsed between this life and the next, where past, present, and future were framed as one. What was bound in the temple was bound in eternity in what the Prophet Joseph Smith termed "sealings."

He called for the Saints "to build unto the Lord a house whereby He could reveal unto His people the ordinances of His house and the glories of His kingdom, and teach the people the way of salvation; for there are certain ordinances and principles that, when they are taught and practiced, must be done in a place or house built for that purpose."[2] He also taught that the whole of mankind stood at the gates of the temple awaiting saving ordinances, and that these rites—long practiced in ancient times—would be returned to God's children in their purity and promise in the Nauvoo Temple.

Below: Hearkening back to ancient times, the Latter-day Saints embraced prophets, revelation, priesthood—and temples. Nauvoo, their gathering place, was never about building a town. Nauvoo was all about building a temple.

JOSEPH SMITH DREW UPON the substance, funds, faith, and zeal of all to fashion the temple. Construction began in the early 1840s when a crew of these religious refugees started chipping away the limestone walls of a Mississippi riverbank on the western edge of Illinois. Like the Israelites of old, these Latter-day Saints were intent on building a house for God—one stone at a time.

The builders had no power tools; they did not fully understand the mathematics of structural engineering; they were farmers and common laborers; they were poor. Through their efforts, much of it volunteer labor and for the most part unskilled, they completed the temple and then used it day and night for only six weeks. Their efforts drew interest; visitors by the dozens streamed into the city to view the grand structure.

A visitor to Nauvoo described the completed temple as "a large and splendid edifice, built on the Egyptian style of architecture," adding he was astonished by "its grandeur and magnificence." *The New York Sun* credited "the Mormon prophet" as being the man who "in the blaze of this nineteenth century" founded a new religion and built "a city, with new laws, institutions, and orders of architecture."

By 1845 the dramatic structure's walls could be seen for more than a mile. The temple—128 feet long, 88 feet wide, 65 feet to the roof, and 165 feet from the ground to the top of the tower's spire—created a town center very different from any other community. It was a curious blend of architectural styles, and a bold statement of a community at odds with its neighbors in social, religious, and cultural practices. Their dazzling white temple was an amazing accomplishment, a phenomenon of their time; yet their efforts had never been intended to make a statement to anyone but God.

Temple construction became a community-bonding enterprise with doctrinal roots Joseph Smith described as "gathering." For six years, thousands of religious converts had steamed up the river, docked at one of the town's wharfs, and stepped into a new life, one centered on gathering to give service to God. That's why they had come. By 1846 they were gone, driven out by neighbors and one-time believers who could not abide the unfolding religion, its prophets, or its people. Nauvoo—the town and its temple—stood silent on the banks of the Mississippi—as the river ripples quietly licked the wounds of war.

On the heels of the Mormons' forced exodus to the desert basins of the Rocky Mountains, arsonists torched the abandoned Nauvoo Temple in 1848. Two years later a tornado toppled the

Above: The original Nauvoo Temple was captured in an 1846 daguerreotype believed to be taken by Lucian Foster.

Left: Tools such as these would have been used by those who worked on the original Nauvoo Temple.

Opposite: The nearly completed temple, its tower piercing the mist and catching the morning sun, stands poised to reclaim its religious prominence.

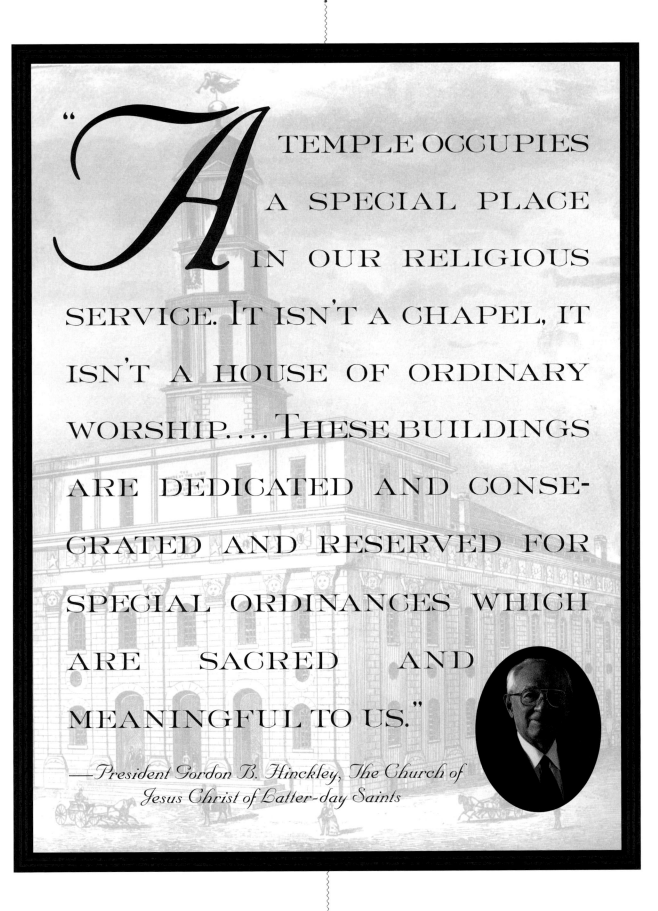

"A TEMPLE OCCUPIES A SPECIAL PLACE IN OUR RELIGIOUS SERVICE. IT ISN'T A CHAPEL, IT ISN'T A HOUSE OF ORDINARY WORSHIP.... THESE BUILDINGS ARE DEDICATED AND CONSECRATED AND RESERVED FOR SPECIAL ORDINANCES WHICH ARE SACRED AND MEANINGFUL TO US."

—*President Gordon B. Hinckley, The Church of Jesus Christ of Latter-day Saints*

walls. The once-proud edifice that spoke of a peculiar people—their faith and sacrifice—was gone.

More than 150 years later, in April of 1999, President Gordon B. Hinckley, fifteenth president of The Church of Jesus Christ of Latter-day Saints, made a surprise announcement regarding the reconstruction of this revered edifice. The rebuilding "says that we are aware and conscious and grateful for a great history that lies behind us," President Hinckley said, "and that we are aware and conscious of a great opportunity and challenge that lies ahead of us. This restoration stands as something of a monument to that maturity in the Church." The construction immediately went on a fast track.

Though temple building has a rich heritage in antiquity, it was an anomaly in religious circles in the nineteenth century with the exception of the Latter-day Saints. The Mormons began to build temples in the Church's infancy; they continued that tradition when they went west in 1847. The completion of the rebuilt Nauvoo Temple will bring to 113 the number of functioning LDS temples around the nation and the world. Nauvoo was the first LDS temple where holy rites and promises were administered to the faithful to prepare them for salvation. And it will continue to fulfill these purposes today.

"The idea that the Latter-day Saints at that time—under such trying circumstances, in such difficult conditions—would have and could have built this extraordinary building and devoted so many of their resources and their energies to this seemingly impractical enterprise is to me astonishing, and it puts them in the tradition of the great temple-building cultures where people give virtually everything to build these great temples."

—Dr. John Lundquist

The rebuilt Nauvoo Temple looks over a still-quiet Nauvoo. Its presence commemorates the past and heralds the future. It stands on the same footprint as it predecessor, replicates the original architectural design, hosts a golden angel atop the tower, and bears a near-perfect match to those original walls—of sacred stone

"On the 21st of September, 2001, I stood on the grounds of the temple and watched the angel Moroni "fly" to the top of the tower by the aid of a crane, an American flag flying from the line. The day was significant in LDS history, for Moroni first visited the young Joseph Smith that day in 1823. More than a century later, Moroni was sweeping through the sky while thunder clouds hung in place. When Moroni was secured on the tower, the sun broke through and the light in the sky was dazzling. I have learned that the temple is all about lighting the way." —Heidi S. Swinton

1

FROM ANCIENT DAYS

"I obligate myself to build as great a temple as ever Solomon did if the Church will back me up." [1]

—Joseph Smith

own through the ages the temple has been considered the center of the universe, a place where God dwells among His children, where men meet God face-to-face. The temple, often dramatic in its architecture and ennobling as a sanctuary for Deity, served the ancients as the centerpiece of the community, the focus of not only worship but life itself. In Egyptian, Greek, and Far Eastern traditions, civilizations built splendid edifices at enormous cost and human effort to pay homage to God. Their architectural

Previous Page: The remarkable pillars of the Egyptian Temple of Luxor reflect spiritual yearnings of an earlier civilization. In 1799 when a division of French soldiers saw the temple for the first time, the whole army came to "a spontaneous halt and burst into applause."

Below: The Parthenon, the chief temple on the rocky Acropolis in Greece, is recognized as one of the architectural marvels of the ages.

Opposite: On the northern shore of the Sea of Galilee rest the ruins of ancient Capernaum. This was where

presence is overshadowed only by the messages communicated by these structures, some still standing. The Nauvoo Temple was no different.

Traditionally, temples were considered the spiritual summit, the closest point to God and His legions, the setting where people could learn the ways of the heavens, receive solemn rites, and commit themselves to the laws of the Almighty. In such consecrated space, people took their bearings

Jesus Christ taught His disciples of the sealing power: "Verily I say unto you, Whatsoever ye shall bind on earth shall be bound in heaven: and whatever ye shall loose on earth shall be loosed in heaven" (Matt. 18:18). Architectural remains feature the Star of David, which is also represented on this early sketch for the Nauvoo Temple windows that were later crafted in colored glass.

"Most religions identify not only special times which may be signified by movement of the stars and the planets in heaven, but also particular space which has to be treated in a way different from and holier than secular space."

—Dr. Jacob Neusner

on the universe and communed with the heavens. Dr. Carol Meyers, explains, "A temple wasn't really a house of worship as such, although there was worship involved in it. But it was first and foremost a kind of palatial residence that would be befitting a powerful deity. The very term 'temple' actually, in at least the Hebrew Bible in the Hebrew text itself, is really 'The House of the Lord.'"

The Great Jehovah of the Old Testament commanded His covenant people to build sacred structures that were more than places to assemble. These enclosures

people, as we know now from the scrolls," observes Dr. Truman G. Madsen, Professor Emeritus, Brigham Young University, "was that there would be eventually a glorious messianic temple to which the Messiah Himself would come."

Dr. Meyers observes, "People believed in their god or gods, and one of the ways in which they felt they could prosper in the world would be to have their god with them, because their god was powerful; it empowered them. And if they took care of their god and their god's needs in this palatial residence, then their hope was that their

THE TERM "TEMPLE" . . . IN THE HEBREW TEXT ITSELF MEANS "THE HOUSE OF THE LORD."

were consecrated for holy purposes and ceremonies. Some of the first temples were natural settings, beginning with the Garden of Eden. Tops of mountains were sacred space for communing with the Lord. For example, the Lord spoke to Moses on Mount Horeb: "Draw not nigh hither: put off thy shoes from off thy feet, for the place whereon thou standest is holy ground"(Ex. 3:5).

The Latter-day Saints of the nineteenth century ascribed to patterns for temples found in the Bible. The Israelites of the Old Testament and New Testament reverenced them, and their descendants who ventured to the Americas built temples with the same intent—to give glory to the Almighty.

God then commanded Moses to direct the Israelites to "make me a sanctuary; that I may dwell among them"(Ex. 25:8). This portable temple-tabernacle served as an ever-moving center for this nomadic people in their sustained pilgrimage to the Promised Land. "The great faith of the Dead Sea

god or the deities would in turn take care of them, provide them with economic prosperity and blessings in the harsh world of antiquity."

Centuries later, David hoped to construct a house for God, but it would be his son Solomon who would be called by the Lord to actually build the temple. King Solomon built atop Mount Zion what was recognized and still is referred to as one of the most remarkable structures of all time, with courts and gates and chambers of magnificent proportion. The "workers of stone" numbered in the thousands; the opportunity to labor on the temple was viewed with great reverence. So extensive and venerated was the stonework on Solomon's Temple that masonry as a profession dates to that era.

Solomon, in dedicating his stone-on-stone temple to the Lord said, "I have surely built thee a house to dwell in, an settled place for thee to abide in for ever"(1 Kgs. 8:13). This remarkable structure stood in Jerusalem for a thousand years,

Below: King Solomon's temple, which stood atop Mount Zion in Jerusalem for a thousand years is recognized as one of the most remarkable structures of all time. So extensive was the stonework on this massive structure, that masonry as a profession dates to that era.

though its purity was compromised early by the iniquity of the people.

Other temples followed. The Temple of Zerubabbel was completed in 515 B.C. and stood for five centuries. Though less showy in materials and design, it was the best the people—recently released from bondage—could build. This was where sacrifices to God were made, where teachings of the Great Creator were elaborated, where the prophets Zechariah, Haggai, and Malachi ministered. Said the Lord through his Prophet

Haggai, "In this place will I give peace"(Hag. 2:9).

During His earthly ministry, Jesus Christ worshiped in the temple constructed by Herod the Great, King of Judea, at Jerusalem. A thousand priests worked on the temple, first reconstructing and then shaping a new structure far more grand than those previously erected. This was the temple where the baby Jesus was presented, where the young boy Jesus taught the priests, and where the ministering Messiah drove money changers from the courtyard.

That temple took forty-six years to complete, and though Herod had designs to bring attention to himself with its grandeur, it was still viewed by the faithful as God's holy house. To them, its glory was dependent not on its size, but on what they believed was its sacred purpose. When the Romans captured Jerusalem in A.D. 70, Herod's magnificent temple was destroyed—leaving not "one stone upon another" (Mark 13:2). The destruction of this temple brought to an end the era of such temple building in the Holy Land.

Temples were not limited to the Old World. The Book of Mormon includes records of a righteous colony who fled Jerusalem before its capture by the Babylonians and established a civilization in the Americas about 588–570 B.C. Their prophet Nephi constructed a temple "after the manner of the temple of Solomon save it were not built of so many precious things" (2 Ne. 5:16). In A.D. 34, Jesus Christ appeared to "a great multitude gathered together" around another Nephite temple in Bountiful (3 Ne. 11:1).

The spectacular cathedrals of the Middle Ages took center stage for worship as Christianity—in various forms—put down roots in Europe. These lofty structures, many of them architectural masterpieces, did not carry the responsibility as earthly homes for the divine; they were used for general church services, public meetings, and education. It was expected that the elaborate stonework, stained glass, paintings, and windows would inspire greater faith in the people.

TEMPLE BUILDING

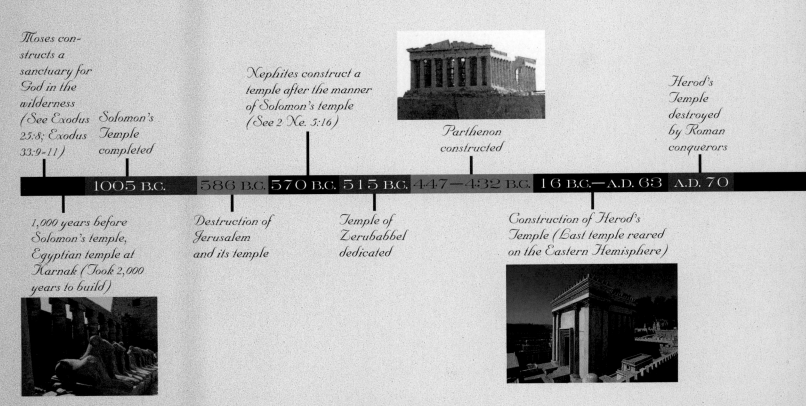

Moses constructs a sanctuary for God in the wilderness (See Exodus 25:8; Exodus 33:9-11)

Solomon's Temple completed

Nephites construct a temple after the manner of Solomon's temple (See 2 Ne. 5:16)

Parthenon constructed

Herod's Temple destroyed by Roman conquerors

| 1005 B.C. | 586 B.C. | 570 B.C. | 515 B.C. | 447–432 B.C. | 16 B.C.—A.D. 63 | A.D. 70 |

1,000 years before Solomon's temple, Egyptian temple at Karnak (Took 2,000 years to build)

Destruction of Jerusalem and its temple

Temple of Zerubbabel dedicated

Construction of Herod's Temple (Last temple reared on the Eastern Hemisphere)

Cathedrals also began to rise in America as cities claimed to come of age. These stone structures followed the grand style of European tradition and spoke of an emerging empowerment in religious circles. Still, there were a vast number of people seeking greater involvement in their own religious experience. This movement in America, described by scholars as the Second Great Awakening, was populated with "seekers" who were looking for something other than the traditional forms of religion. Words like "reformation," "restoration," "ancient order of things," and "revelation" were well-worn topics of discussion.

The viewpoint of New Englander Theodore Parker reflected that of many: "I knew that I had thoroughly broken with the ecclesiastical authority of Christiandom; its God was not my God, nor its scriptures my word of God, nor its Christ my Savior; for I preferred the Jesus of historic fact to the Christ of theologic fancy. Its narrow, partial, and unnatural heaven I did not wish to enter on the terms proposed, nor did I fear, since earliest youth, its mythic, roomy hell, wherein the tribune of God, with his pack of devils to aid, tore the human race in pieces forever and ever."[2]

In a celebrated address to the Divinity College of Cambridge Massachusetts, Ralph Waldo Emerson stirred the school of thought stating, "Historical Christianity has fallen into the error that corrupts all attempts to communicate religion," and he pressed the students to "acquaint men at first hand with Deity."[3]

But it was not a graduate of a hallowed institution or a cleric of renown that would step forward to unite heaven and

THROUGH THE AGES

AUGUST 3:
Placement of cornerstone for a future temple at Independence, Jackson County, Missouri

JULY 23:
Kirtland cornerstone-laying ceremony

JULY 4:
Cornerstones laid for temple at Far West

APRIL 6:
Approximately 10,000 people attend the laying of the four cornerstones of the Nauvoo Temple

MAY 24:
Nauvoo capstone laid under the direction of President Brigham Young

FEB. 4:
Latter-day Saints begin pilgrimage west

OCT. 9:
Arsonist torches Nauvoo Temple

APRIL 4:
Pres. Hinckley announces plans to rebuild Nauvoo Temple

NOV. 5:
Cornerstone Ceremony

| 1831 | 1833 | 1836 | 1838 | 1841 | 1844 | 1845 | 1846 | 1848 | 1850 | 1999 | 2000 | 2002 |

JUNE
Kirtland Temple site dedicated

MARCH 27:
Kirtland Temple dedicated

JAN. 19:
Revelation commanding the Saints to erect a temple in Nauvoo

JUNE 27:
Prophet Joseph Smith and his brother Hyrum are martyred at Carthage Jail

DEC. 10:
Temple work begins in the Nauvoo Temple

MAY 1:
Nauvoo Temple dedicated by Elders Orson Hyde and Wilford Woodruff

MAY 27:
Tornado topples temple walls

OCT. 24:
Temple ground-breaking

JUNE 27-30:
Dedication of rebuilt Nauvoo Temple

earth—with a temple. It was a bold and believing Joseph Smith, son of a New England farmer, who would be called to speak for God as his latter-day prophet. He reported talking with God the Father and His Son, Jesus Christ, when they appeared to him in a grove in upstate New York. Other manifestations followed, and an early revelation received by Joseph declared, "This generation shall have my word through you." Heavenly visitations were his hallmark. Joseph said that an angel named Moroni revealed to him, "God had a work for me to do, and that my name should be had for good and evil among all nations, kindreds and tongues" (JS–H 1:33).

That work unfolded quickly. In the spring of 1829, Joseph received the power of the Aaronic Priesthood of God from John the Baptist, and the Melchizedek Priesthood from the early apostles Peter, James, and John; and he also published the Book of Mormon, new scriptures bearing witness of Jesus Christ, which he had translated from gold plates given him by the angel Moroni. On April 6, 1830, the twenty-four-year-old Smith and a handful of close

"I saw two personages, whose brightness and glory defy all description, standing above me in the air. One of them . . . said, pointing to the other—'This is My Beloved Son. Hear Him!'"

—JOSEPH SMITH

followers established a church, and within the year he and many of the converts to this restored religion moved to Kirtland, Ohio.

In July 1830, Joseph Smith announced to Church members that the Lord had directed them to build a temple. "The first great object before us, and the saints generally, is to help forward the completion of the Temple," he announced. "For God requires of His Saints to build Him a house wherein his servants may be instructed and endowed with power from on high."[4] He later would refer to temple building as "a work that God and angels have contemplated with delight for generations past; that fired the souls of the ancient patriarchs and prophets, a work that is destined to bring about the destruction of the powers of darkness, the renovation of the earth, the glory of God, and the salvation of the human family."[5] That connection with heaven and its authority was what so many had been seeking.

Dr. Jacob Neusner explains, "Mormon restorationism was aimed at recovering the correct model of the temple that God had instruct-

"JOSEPH SMITH WAS BORN IN 1805 IN VERMONT IN A RURAL ENVIRONMENT. HE WAS NOT BORN INTO AN ENVIRONMENT OF SCHOLARSHIP OR RESEARCH LIBRARIES SUCH AS WE HAVE AVAILABLE TO US TODAY. AND YET THE MORMON TEMPLE AS IT WAS REVEALED TO HIM . . . EXHIBITS, AND REFLECTS AND REPRODUCES THE GREAT ANCIENT CHARACTERISTICS OF THE TEMPLE AS WE CAN KNOW THEM THROUGH STUDY. AND SO THERE ARE MANY FEATURES OF THE MORMON TEMPLE WHICH WERE REVEALED TO [JOSEPH SMITH] BUT WHICH MATCH AS IT WERE THE PRACTICES OF THE GREAT, ANCIENT TEMPLE-BUILDING CULTURES SUCH AS EGYPT."

—Dr. John M. Lundquist

ed the Israelites to create. This is comparable to the aspiration of the Jewish people to restore the temple rites in an accurate and correct way when the Messiah comes and signals the rebuilding of the temple."

Observed Ohio resident Frederic G. Mather, "The advent of several hundred strangers into the midst of the insignificant hamlet was an event of considerable importance, but when they selected a most commanding site, of easy access to the public highway, and commenced the building of a church, all Northern Ohio looked on in wonder."[6]

In Kirtland, the young prophet recognized the hand of God in all things, even building a temple. Some members suggested building a log structure; others favored a frame building. "Shall we," countered Joseph Smith, "build a house for our God, of logs? No, I have a better plan than that. I have a plan of the house of the Lord, given by himself; and you will soon see by this, the difference between our calculation and his idea of things."[7] Though it was described as resembling in design a New England chapel with a general meeting area, Joseph Smith called the temple "a house of prayer, a house of fasting, a house of faith, a house of learning, a house of glory, a house of order, a house of God" (D&C 88:119).

Construction of the Kirtland Temple began on June 6, 1833, and took three years to complete. "Great exertions were made to expedite the work of the Lord's house, and notwithstanding it was commenced almost with nothing, as to means, yet the way opened as we proceeded, and the saints rejoiced."[8]

The temple was built at great cost—in labor, finances, and community support. These seekers-turned-Latter-day Saints did not integrate well with their neighbors, and some who initially embraced the new religion turned away and became bitter foes. Mobs threatened to destroy the temple or at least slow the work.

The way Joseph Smith described the Kirtland Temple held a mystique that captured the imagination of the people. "Finish that temple and God will fill it with power," said the young prophet.[9] The completion of the temple brought with it the

Above: In four different locations—in Ohio, Missouri, and Illinois—Joseph Smith dedicated land to build temples. Of those, only the temples in Kirtland, Ohio, and Nauvoo, Illinois, were completed. In the Kirtland Temple, dedicated March 27, 1836 by the Prophet Joseph Smith, ancient prophets restored priesthood keys making it possible for sacred work to be performed in LDS temples beginning with Nauvoo. Photo ca. 1907.

promised spiritual manifestations. Members of the Church spoke of seeing visions—heavenly messengers in at least ten different meetings; at five gatherings different people claimed they had beheld the Savior Himself.

Of a January 1836 meeting in the temple at Kirtland, the Prophet Joseph Smith recorded: "The heavens were opened upon us and I beheld the celestial kingdom of God, and the glory thereof." He related seeing "the blazing throne of

appeared to some, while a sense of divine presence was realized by all present, and each heart was filled with 'joy inexpressible and full of glory.'"[13] So consuming was the spiritual experience that for several hours the people did not wish to leave.

The occasion has been described as similar to the Day of Pentecost. "It couldn't happen that Christ could come and there would be a saintly people ready to receive Him, unless they were prepared through the temple," claims Dr. Truman

"Joseph Smith was convinced that the culmination of human history and of sacred history and the preparation for the millennium could not really come to pass in fullness unless the people were prepared through temples."

—DR. TRUMAN G. MADSEN

God" and "the beautiful streets of that kingdom, which had the appearance of being paved with gold." Of that evening he concluded that many in his company "saw the face of the Savior" and that "all communed with the heavenly host."[10]

The days surrounding the dedication of the Kirtland Temple were filled with "glorious visions." George A. Smith spoke of "being moved upon by an invisible power."[11] Frederick G. Williams bore witness to seeing the Savior, and David Whitmer recounted seeing three angels passing up the south aisle.[12]

"No mortal language can describe the heavenly manifestations of that memorable day," wrote Eliza R. Snow. "A pillar of light was several times seen resting down upon the roof," she said. "Angels

Madsen. "That was the undergirding motivation both of the prophet and of the people."

The Kirtland Temple served as a preparatory temple for the one to follow in Nauvoo. On Easter Sunday, April 3, 1836, Joseph Smith said he received a series of visions in which ancient prophets Moses, Elias, and Elijah returned to him "the keys of the authority" to administer in all rites to be performed in temples. In Joseph Smith's recorded prayer of dedication of the temple, he reiterated the hope of those who had worshiped in a temple since antiquity: "That all people who shall enter upon the threshold of the Lord's house may feel thy power, and feel constrained to acknowledge that thou hast sanctified it, and that it is thy house, a place of thy holiness"(D&C 109:13).

By 1838, the Church was beset with apostasy from within and persecution from without, and Joseph's followers abandoned their temple in Kirtland, joining with Saints in Missouri who had been forced from their homes as well.

It was common practice in the mid-nineteenth century for groups to unite against others they did not like, of whose practices or ideas they did not approve. In the eyes of their detractors, the Mormons seemed to be going against the prevailing common values, common assumptions, common Judeo-Christian heritage. Within months, Joseph Smith was imprisoned, the property of the Saints was confiscated, and an order to exterminate the Mormons was

---

"OTHER RELIGIONS WERE RIDICULED IN AMERICAN SOCIETY, BUT NO OTHER RELIGION WAS AS PERSECUTED AS MORMONS."

—*Dr. John Butler*

---

signed by Governor Boggs. In the harsh winter months of 1838, eight to ten thousand men, women, and children fled nearly two hundred miles east to Illinois. "We took up our march towards the rising sun," wrote Nancy Naomi Alexander Tracy. "It stormed continually."[14] John Hammer recalled the march to the Mississippi River valley. "Our family, as well as many others, were almost barefooted, and some had to wrap their feet in cloths in order to keep them from freezing and protect them from the sharp points of the frozen ground. This, at best, was very imperfect protection, and often the blood from our feet marked the frozen earth."[15] They found refuge in Illinois and began to gather. Again.

The ANG

"The [Nauvoo] temple on the exterior is a re-creation of what was there once, just as nearly as we can make it, except for one thing and that's the Moroni figure on the top," President Gordon B. Hinckley explained. "The original temple had a recumbent figure resting horizontally, a weather vane style figure. We looked at that very carefully and studied it very thoughtfully. Every other temple that we've built [that carries that figure] has the figure Moroni erect. And after much deliberation we concluded to make that change to put an erect angel rather than the recumbent angel."

The figure was placed Sept. 21, 2001, in commemoration of the 178th anniversary of Moroni's first appearance to Joseph Smith. The LDS Church "flew three angels" that day: one in Nauvoo, Illinois; one in Boston, Massachusetts; and one in The Hague, Netherlands. The LDS Church teaches that Moroni was the last of the prophet-leaders in the Western Hemisphere whose history is recorded in the Book of Mormon. Latter-day Saints believe John the Revelator foretold Moroni's angelic ministry: "And I saw another angel fly in the midst of heaven, having the everlasting gospel to preach unto them that dwell on the earth, and to every nation, and kindred, and tongue, and people"(Rev. 14:6).

According to tradition, the original tower would have been finished with a lightning rod, but the Prophet Joseph rejected that finishing touch stating, "if God, who now holds the lightnings in his hands chooses to direct a thunderbolt against those solid walls and demolish the building, it is his affair."[16] The angel atop the weather vane was perhaps a compromise. Perrigrine Sessions observed, "They raised the vane which is a representation of an angel in his priestly robes with a Book of Mormon in one hand and a trumpet in the other which [was] over laid with gold leaf."[17]

The editor of the *Carthage Republican* described the figure as "winging as a sort of wind-vane above

EL MORONI

the spire." He relates, "we climbed to the top of that vast dome and planting our feet around the lofty rod which supported the bronze angel, we viewed a scene of magnificence vast and varied in its scope—the immense river half circling the beautiful city, the towns and villages that dotted its shores for miles in either direction, the tasteful farms that stretched their uninterrupted lines of hedge and fence into the misty distance, and the grim cannon and the men who guarded them, shrunken into pop-guns and pigmies so far below our feet. Such is our recollection of the great city and its proud temple in 1846."[18]

Right: Sculptor Karl Quilter first sketched the Moroni image, then shaped the statue in clay. The finished figure was cast in fiberglass. Quilter has created many of the angels that stand on LDS temple spires.

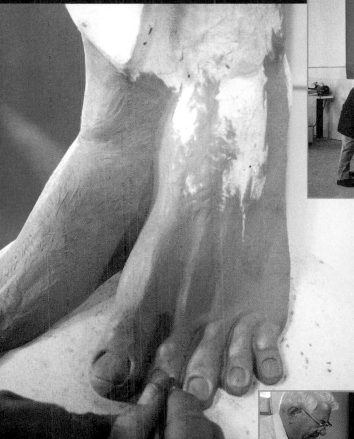

Left: Moroni stands six-feet ten-inches atop a ball symbolizing the world. The first standing angel was placed on the Salt Lake Temple spire and was called the Angel of the Restoration.

Above: The completed statue was shipped from Salt Lake City, Utah, in a massive pine box. Inside, the figure was secured to wood panels at the top of the head and at the bottom of the globe to prevent anything from touching the gold leaf.

Left: On September 21, 2001—the 178th anniversary of Moroni's first appearance to Joseph Smith—a Moroni statue was placed on the tower of the Nauvoo Temple. Two other Moroni statues were positioned that day on LDS temples in Boston, Massachusetts, and The Hague, Netherlands.

Above: Two layers of gold leaf are meticulously applied to the fiberglass statue by LaVar Walgren. The exceptionally thin 24-carat gold is brushed on by hand and is expected to last fifteen years.

on the Nauvoo Temple

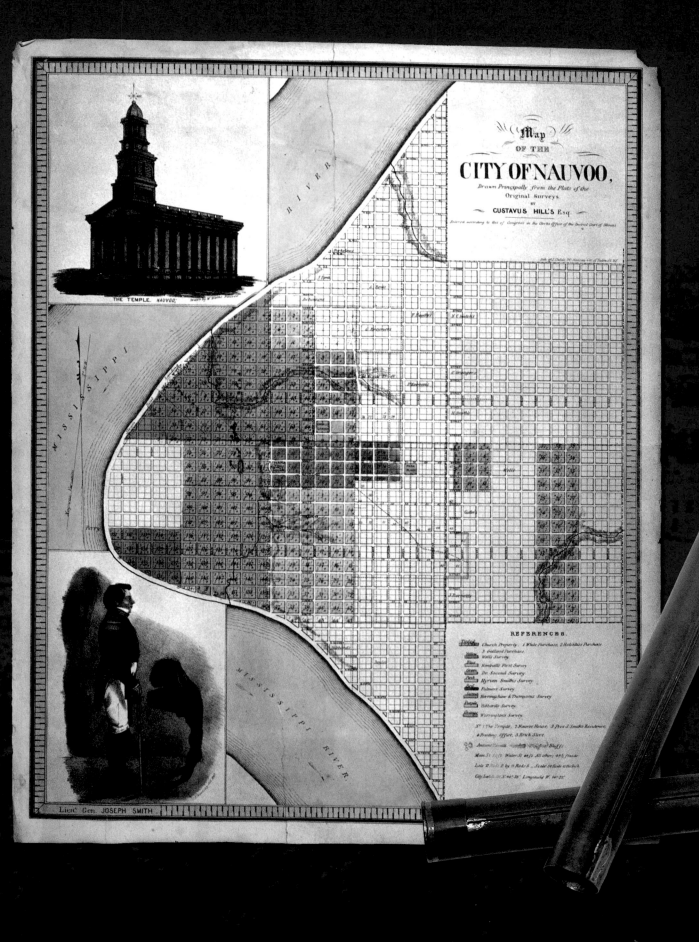

2

BUILDING THE KINGDOM

"We need the Temple more

than anything else." [1]

— Joseph Smith

In the winter of 1839, nearly five thousand men, women, and children straggled into Quincy, Illinois, having been threatened with extermination by the Governor of Missouri, the state next door. Many had lost their homes and farms; some had lost their loved ones. They left behind their beloved prophet, Joseph Smith, and a handful of his close associates in a dungeon called Liberty Jail. In April he and the others would be allowed to "escape" and Joseph would make his way to Illinois to join his people.

LIBERTY JAIL

Settling on the very fringes of a growing nation, these adherents to this newfound religion had clashed repeatedly with their neighbors in state after state. They were focused on preparing for the Second Coming, the Millennium, the word of God—a sharp contrast to the economic pursuits of other settlers. They worked together in a climate that otherwise fostered personal independence, and they traded with each other rather than their neighbors, prompting a rift no matter where they tried to settle. In both Ohio and Missouri, the Latter-day Saints escaped with little more than their lives, leaving behind homes, farms, and hopes for fulfilling the divine command to build a temple for God. The *Quincy Whig* wrote of the sorry plight of the refugees: "A heavy sin lies somewhere in between the leaders of this misguided sect and the Missourians, it is difficult to fix the responsibility."[2]

Looking back at that era, current mayor of Quincy, Charles W. Scholz, suggests, "In 1839 there were about 1,500 people here in Quincy. And those settlers welcomed 5,000 Mormons that had been forcibly driven from the state of Missouri under harsh winter conditions, had walked across the frozen Mississippi. And, they were offered food and clothing and shelter. Now to put that in perspective, that would be like the 42,000 residents of Quincy today taking care of 150,000 refugees. . . . That is one of the most incredible acts of humanity, I think, in the history of this country."

By late spring of 1839, Joseph Smith had secured property on a boggy horseshoe bend of the Mississippi 40 miles upriver from Quincy, and 190 miles from St. Louis, and set to work building a town. He called it Nauvoo. It eventually would prove to be the Mormons' last stand in America, "the land of the free." But first, they would make their case to build the kingdom of God on earth with a temple as the centerpiece.

Nauvoo was where they hoped to learn and live their Christian doctrine, prepare for the Second Coming of the Lord, and find strength and comfort in each other's company. Joseph Smith was convinced that such purpose and peace was available to the people only if they had a temple. He looked "forward with pleasing anticipation to the future," expecting to soon "see the thousands of Israel flocking to this region in obedience to the heavenly command; numerous inhabitants—Saints—thickly studding the flowery and wide-spread prairies of Illinois; temples for the worship of our God erecting in various parts, and great peace resting upon Israel."[3]

Oliver B. Huntington spoke the sentiment of the faithful. "We quickly resolved, we will stay here as long as Joseph wants us to—he knows what is best!"[4]

"We were again to start anew to make another home with nothing but our hands and brains to begin with," Nancy Naomi Alexander Tracy wrote of the time. "We were not

VIEW OF QUINCY AND MISSISSIPPI BOTTOM
FROM COL. MAYES IN MARION COUNTY, MO.

conquered in spirit but determined to live our religion and stand by the principles of the Gospel and help to build up the kingdom of God on the earth."[5]

Dr. John Lundquist explains: "God chooses someone to be his prophet, to be his mouthpiece on earth for his people. . . . And the building of the temple is part of that whole process. One of the things that is revealed is the temple."

Above: A Quincy newspaper said of the Mormon refugees, "If they have been thrown upon our shores destitute, through the oppressive people of Missouri, common humanity must oblige us to aid and relieve them."[6]

Joseph first began talking of a temple in Nauvoo in 1840, but the work did not begin until he announced in 1841 that God had commanded, "build a house unto me"(D&C 124:31). He called for the "speedy erection" of a temple upon which "great blessings depend" and praised "the zeal which is manifested by the Saints."[7] French philosopher Hyppolite Taine observed, "These exiles thought that they were founding the city of God, the

"WHEN JOSEPH SAID, 'THIS IS THE WILL OF THE LORD,' THAT WAS AS IF PETER HIMSELF HAD SPOKEN."

—Dr. Truman G. Madsen

"It was the temple that gave Nauvoo
its meaning. It was the temple that made
Nauvoo different than other
American cities of the time."

—Dr. Glen M. Leonard

metropolis of mankind. They considered themselves the renovators of the world."[8]

The rise of this religious enclave was dramatic. What began as an uninviting marshland became, in the next five years, a hub of activity. Mormons straddled the Mississippi with settlements in Nauvoo on the Illinois side and Montrose on the Iowa shore. Eliza R. Snow observed that Nauvoo "seemed to have been held in reserve to meet the occasion, for none but Saints full of faith, and trusting in the power of God could have established that city."[9]

Joseph Smith rallied the members to this

plated with delight, for generations past; that fired the souls of the ancient patriarchs and prophets—a work that is destined to bring about the destruction of the powers of darkness, the renovation of the earth, the glory of God, and salvation of the human family."[10]

And so, as the Mormons began to put down roots in Illinois, they also began to put up the walls of a temple. This "modern structure," an 1843 visitor wrote to his home newspaper, the *Pittsburgh Gazette*, was intended "to revive

"IT HAS BEEN SAID BY AN OBSERVER OF MORMON HISTORY THAT IT'S ONE THING TO FIND A DEDICATED INDIVIDUAL; IT'S ANOTHER TO FIND A CONSECRATED COMMUNITY. AND THE COMMUNITY OF SAINTS IN NAUVOO WERE A CONSECRATED COMMUNITY, BOTH TO THE BUILDING OF THAT TEMPLE AND THEN TO THE RECEIVING WITHIN IT."

—*Dr. Truman G. Madsen*

singular "cause of Christ" with eloquence:

"Our children will rise up and call us blessed; and generations yet unborn will dwell with peculiar delight upon the scenes that we have passed through, the privations that we have endured; the untiring zeal that we have manifested; the insurmountable difficulties that we have overcome in laying the foundation of a work that brought about the glory and blessings which they will realize; a work that God and angels have contem-

the departed glories of the temple of Jerusalem, and . . . is apparently dear to every Mormon heart, as was that famous and venerated house of the devout Jew."[11]

The Saints were determined to follow the counsel of their prophet, and willingly gave of their meager means in their labors to build a temple. Accounts of families and their scant foodstuffs and difficult living conditions are legion. Wrote John Pulsipher, "The Lord gave a commandment that a Temple should be built to His name. It seemed almost impossible for so poor a people to build such a temple in their poverty, but the Lord never requires more of men than they can perform if they will go to with their might and trust in Him."[12] Many voiced that in sacrificing for the Lord's house they knew they would be blessed immeasurably. "It was the desire of my heart to serve God and keep His commandments in adversity and prosperity," William Adams said. "The prophet was very anxious to have the temple finished so the Saints could receive their endowments."[13]

SHEER NUMBERS POURING into Nauvoo gave the city stature in the rapid expansion of the state of Illinois. In less than five years this Mississippi river town with a religious twist was considered one of the largest cities in the state and a stronghold of political votes. But it was the temple, not the numbers, that drew visitors from other communities and other states. Four or five steamboats a day from towns strung up and down the river stopped at the Mormon wharf to view what was essentially a massive public works project going up on the hill.

Above: Missouri citizens accused the Saints of voting as a block and swinging elections. Such political clout created strong resentment among the locals who were already apprehensive about the Mormons' growing economic position from land holdings and trade, and because they exchanged mostly with each other.

Far Above: The Temple was a dramatic sight to visitors; to the Saints it was sacred space protected by stone walls.

Above: From the Iowa Mormon settlements on the Mississippi, the Saints could see the progress of temple construction.

Right: In 1846, the town of Nauvoo rivaled Chicago as the largest city in Illinois. Today, homes and shops are being restored.

The best space in the settlement would be selected . . .

A place where God's presence would easily come to rest.

Even the placement of the temple was significant. The Nauvoo Temple was on the bluff overlooking the river and the surrounding farms. Such sacred space has roots in ancient times. "As a city, as a settlement grew . . . it needed to have its own temple, its own sacred space," Dr. Carol Meyers contends. "The best space in the settlement would be selected—the highest top part of the city, the one with the best view or the best breeze, because after all a temple, as a house for God, people would want it to be in the most beneficial location . . . a place where God's presence would easily come to rest."

Temple building was not new to the Mormons, nor was the tension that seemed to accompany their efforts. They had completed a "House of God" in Ohio, one preparatory to the purpose of the Nauvoo Temple, and had been forced to leave it. They had dedicated two temple sites in Missouri—at Independence and Far West—all with the desire "that the Son of Man might have a place to manifest himself to his people" (D&C 109:5). They had been forced from those locations before building could begin. Their devotion to the cause was made even more curious by revelation that commanded the people to "Build a house to my name, for the Most High to dwell therein . . . prove . . . faithful in all things . . . that I may reveal mine ordinances . . . unto my people . . . and crown you with honor, immortality and eternal life" (D&C 124:27, 55).

While the Mormons believed that their work on the temple was divinely inspired, visitors simply marveled at the feat of such a structure in an obscure little town. Boston native Josiah Quincy, who was perfectly familiar with some of the nation's grand religious and government buildings, toured the unfinished temple in June 1844 with Joseph Smith as his guide. Quincy suggested the temple was "a wonderful structure altogether indescribable." And in his opinion, the temple could not "be compared to any ecclesiastical building."[14] Quincy's comments reflect that he did not understand the premise of the development of the town and its inhabitants' preoccupation with the temple. He saw instead a city "with its wide streets sloping gracefully to the farms enclosed on the prairie" and suggested this industry "seemed to be a better Temple to Him who prospers the work of industrious hands."[15]

In time, the Mormons' fiercely independent Illinois neighbors became wary of these new settlers who subscribed to a religious theocracy. The clash of cultures emerged slowly, drawing battle

> "THE TEMPLE WAS WHERE ALL THE HOPES OF THE SAINTS RESTED. THAT'S WHERE ALL THE ASPIRATIONS POINTED, TO THAT BUILDING AND THAT SITE. . . . I BELIEVE THAT GROUND IS SACRED GROUND."
>
> —*President Gordon B. Hinckley*

lines that eventually erupted in war. Nehemiah in the Old Testament spoke of carrying on what was considered the work of God to reconstruct the walls of Jerusalem under the threat of attack. As Nehemiah described it: "While the building was going on, none of us took off our clothes; each kept his weapon in his hand."[16] President Brigham Young spoke of Nauvoo in similar terms: "But what of the temple of Nauvoo? By the aid of sword in one hand, and trowel and hammer in the other, with fire arms at hand, and a strong band of police, and the blessings of heaven, the Saints, through hunger and thirst, and weariness, and watchings, and prayings, completed the temple."[17]

This boomtown on the river lived a short life. In six years, what was once a little-inhabited marshland had attracted residents by the thousands. They built homes, farms, and shops. But unlike most settlers and emigrants, they didn't come for the promise of land or business. They came to worship as had their pilgrim forefathers to the New England shores.

Eventually the Mormons were run out of their town and their country. The building of a grand edifice did not spark the hatred and aggression, but its imposing and glittering presence on the muddy Mississippi fed the flames. This stone-on-stone temple stood as a measure of the beliefs of a beleaguered people. The Mormons were not making a statement to their neighbors of their coming of age or their desire for place; rather, they were reflecting the core of belief that had gathered them from distant cities and even countries. They saw themselves as God's children promised "power from on high." The temple would be the setting for elaborating their full fidelity, sanctification, and salvation. For all time. That belief prompted their devotion, sacrifice, and service at the temple site on the hill.

3

NO MATTER THE SACRIFICE

"Many times I have worked on the stone quarry on the banks of the Mississippi River, and had nothing for dinner but cornbread when dry dipped in the river, and worked drilling rock day after day as cheerful and contented as ever I was in my life."[1]

—James Leithead

egrouping on the banks of the Mississippi was not easy. That first summer so many died from fever bred in the wetlands that authorities preached a general funeral sermon every Monday and Thursday. "Death became so frequent a visitor in Nauvoo that we were perfectly familiar with it," wrote Caroline Crosby.[2]

Accounts of near brushes with death were legion, as illustrated in the case of Elijah Fordham, a convert from New York, who lay on his deathbed when Joseph arrived at his door, July 22, 1839. Wrote Wilford Woodruff of the incident:

> As Jesus healed all the sick around Him in His day, so Joseph, the Prophet of God, healed all around on this occasion. He healed all in his house and dooryard, then in company with Sidney Rigdon and several of the Twelve, he went among the sick lying on the bank of the river and he commanded them in a loud voice, in the name of Jesus Christ, to come up and be made whole, and they were all healed.

> When he healed all that were sick on the east side of the river, they crossed the Mississippi river in a ferry-boat to the west side, to Montrose . . . and entered Brother Fordham's house. Brother Fordham had been dying for an hour, and we expected each minute would be his last. I felt the power of God that was overwhelming His Prophet.

> When we entered the House, Brother Joseph walked up to Brother Fordham, and took him by the right hand; in his left hand he held his hat. He saw that Brother Fordham's eyes were glazed, and that he was speechless and unconscious. After taking hold of his hand, he

"Death became so frequent a visitor in Nauvoo, that we were perfectly familiar with it."

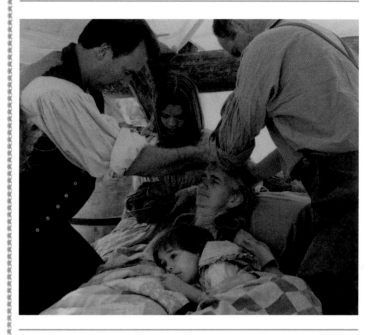

looked down into the dying man's face and said: "Brother Fordham, do you not know me?" At first he made no reply; but we could all see the effect of the Spirit of God resting upon him.

He again said: "Elijah, do you not know me?"

With a low whisper, Brother Fordham answered, "Yes!"

The Prophet then said, "Have you not faith to be healed?"

The answer, which was a little plainer than before, was: "I am afraid it is too late. If you had come sooner, I think I might have been." He had the appearance of a man waking from sleep. It was the sleep of death.

Joseph then said: "Do you believe that Jesus is the Christ?"

"I do, Brother Joseph," was the response.

Then the Prophet of God spoke with a loud voice, as in the majesty of the Godhead: "Elijah, I command you, in the name of Jesus of Nazareth, to arise and be made whole!" The words of the Prophet were not like the words of man, but like the voice of God. It seemed to me that the house shook from its foundation. Elijah leaped from his bed like a man raised from the dead. A healthy color came to his face, and life was manifested in every act. His feet were done up in Indian meal poultices. He kicked them off his feet, scattered the contents, and then called for his clothes and put them on. He asked for a bowl of bread and milk, and ate it; then put on his hat and followed us into the street, to visit others who were sick.[3]

Elijah Fordham went on to play a significant role in the construction of the temple.

A little over a year later, on January 19, 1841, Joseph Smith announced, "The time has now come, when it is necessary to erect a house of prayer, a house of order, a house for the worship of our God."[4] In that temple, he said, the Lord would reveal to his Church sacred priesthood rites and other crucial matters—"things which have been kept hid from before the foundation of the world, things that pertain to the dispensation of the fulness of times,"—things that could only be taught or performed in a temple (D&C 124:41).

Joseph placed responsibility on the shoulders of the people, asking them "to weigh the importance" of the temple "as though the whole labor depended on themselves alone.

"MOST AMERICAN COMMUNITIES WOULD NOT HAVE HAD THE MAJOR PUBLIC BUILDING BE A RELIGIOUS BUILDING. IT WOULD NOT HAVE BEEN A CHURCH . . . . THE FACT THAT YOU HAVE THE TEMPLE BEING THE MAJOR BUILDING, NOT THE COURTHOUSE, NOT THE CITY HALL, NOT A COMMERCIAL BUILDING IS, I THINK, REALLY UNIQUE. ESPECIALLY THE WAY IT IS SITED IN NAUVOO WHERE IT JUST DOMINATES EVERYTHING."

—Dr. Loren N. Horton

By so doing they will emulate the glorious deeds of the fathers, and secure the blessings of heaven upon themselves and their posterity to the latest generation."[5] They began building a temple before they had a meeting hall—before many of them even had homes.

The Nauvoo Temple would dominate both the landscape and the lives of the residents. It would stand as the culmination of Joseph Smith's ministry. As Dr. John Lundquist explains, "The temple-building peoples do not simply go out and start building temples. They are instructed to do so by divine revelation as they perceive that. The Latter-day Saints were . . . called to be this chosen people of God through accepting the gospel and being baptized."

The temple-building effort in Nauvoo was more than a demonstration of the spiritual strivings of the people; it was an expression of their willingness to sacrifice all they had—time, goods, strength, funds—for God. And they had little.

The Saints' self-denial is evidenced in a statement by Christopher Layton as he wrote of his less-than-modest circumstances. "The first winter we had quilts for doors, we had a dirt floor, and when the beds were made down they just about filled the room."[6] Young Louisa Decker watched her mother "sell things that they could scarcely spare" including her best china dishes and fine bed quilt "to donate her part."[7] Many gave cows, horses, wagons, beef, pork, grain, or garden produce for the temple laborers and their families to use.

Stephen Markham, a convert from New York, had sold his property and business in the east for a considerable sum, and moved to Nauvoo. He brought with him a bag of gold. After listening to the Prophet call for contributions to build the Nauvoo Temple, he strode forward at the close of the meeting, put his bag of gold on the rostrum, and announced, "Use this for the temple!" He left the meeting penniless, but being an astute businessman, he was soon able to give additional funds to the Prophet. He later became a colonel of the Nauvoo Legion and a bodyguard to Joseph Smith.[8]

The principle of sacrifice is tied to temple worship. It has always been so. "The ancient temple was a place of sacrifice using the firstlings of the flocks and the firstfruits of the field," Dr. Carol Meyers

> "THEY HAD WHAT THEY CONSIDERED TO BE A REVELATION FROM ON HIGH THAT SAID, 'IF YOU HAVE POWER TO BUILD IT, IT WILL BE BECAUSE YOU KEEP MY COMMANDMENTS, AND IF YOU DO NOT THEN THE LOVE OF THE FATHER WILL NOT CONTINUE WITH YOU AND YOU WILL WALK IN DARKNESS.' NOW, THAT'S PRETTY STRONG. AND THOUGH THEY DIDN'T UNDERSTAND FULLY WHY A TEMPLE WAS CRUCIAL TO THEIR SPIRITUAL LIVES THEY ACCEPTED THAT AND THEY WENT TO WORK AND BUILT IT."
>
> —Dr. Truman G. Madsen

MORMON TEMPLE
NAUVOO, ILLINOIS, 1841–1845

*"Of all the American churches pictured on old blue china
and listed as Staffordshire ware, the rarest is
the Mormon Temple, Potter J(oseph) Twigg,
Kilnhurst Old Pottery, England, 1839–1866."
(from The New York Historical Society Quarterly
July, 1949, p. 185 and January, 1950, pp. 21–22.)*

suggests. "Some today think the temple therefore is good riddance, that it was, to put it starkly, a slaughterhouse. Well, the law of sacrifice applies in a different way. We give ourselves and we give a broken heart and a contrite spirit, at which point we then are in communion with God."

The remarks made by a correspondent for the *New York Herald* underscore this sentiment. Saying that the holy men and great thinkers of the day could well take a lesson from Joseph Smith, the writer suggested that the young prophet had "hit the nail exactly

about 50 masons and stone cutters engaged about the temple," reported the *St. Louis Republican*. "It will be the most extraordinary building on the American continent."[10]

Dr. Glen Leonard explains it this way: "The Mormons could sacrifice to build a temple because they were covenant people. They had promised the Lord in their baptism that they would remember Him, keep His commandments and do what He wanted. When He said, 'Build me a temple,' they said, 'Well, you have given us everything we've got, everything we have comes from you, we'll give you back ten percent.' It was

"As a man of intellectual curiosity, he studied, he learned, he observed, but . . . as far as I am aware, the ultimate source for his information on the temple can only have come through revelation, because such information as is reflected in the Mormon temple was not available to him at that time through study or research." —Dr. John M. Lundquist

on the head, by uniting faith and practice—fancy and fact—religion and philosophy—heaven and earth—so as to form the term of a new religious civilization, bound together in love and tolerance—in industry and energy—that may revolutionize the whole earth one of these days."[9]

That unity of faith and practice was demonstrated in the building of the Nauvoo Temple. Such a massive undertaking for an outpost like Nauvoo drew attention and scrutiny. "There are

a tithing of ten percent of their time and of their resources that built the Nauvoo temple."

The intended structure was massive by most standards and certainly far exceeded any building effort underway for hundreds of miles. Joseph Smith selected young architect William Weeks to design the temple but retained the role as chief architect. At one point, the two clashed regarding the design of round windows in the broad side of the building. Weeks contended

Opposite: Architect William Weeks (1813–1900) sketched this ink-and-graphite rendering of interior capitals and decorative detail for the Nauvoo Temple. Also shown are drafting tools used by stonecutter Francis Clark (1809–1853). The flat, lead template was employed to create intricate spiral- and scroll-shaped patterns that were cut in the capitals of the Temple. The texture of the limestone blocks made tooling easy. Many of the stones were ornamented with basketweave and striation patterns.

Below: Colonial glass in the reconstructed temple is from a factory in Saint Just, France. Blowing glass without using molds is a centuries-old art. A hollow iron pipe is dipped in molten glass, some of which sticks to the pear-shaped end, and is called St. Gobain glass. A master glassblower then gently blows through the pipe until the glass bulges and forms a hollow bulb, which is stretched and twirled.

Left: This master glassblower, third generation at his art, shapes the glass into a cylinder, called a "muff."

Above: The muffs are allowed to cool, then one side of the muff is scored from end to end and separated. The muff is reheated in a kiln to approximately 600° Farenheit, where the soft glass begins to sag. The craftsman then reaches in with a long piece of poplar wood and flattens the cylinder into a flat sheet. After a one-hour cool down, the sheet is then trimmed square and is ready to cut into panes.

Charles Allen explains that the paint for the window sashes was manufactured in Holland and is renowned for a consistency of straight pigments and resins that ensure luster and longevity. Each window was finished with hand-brushed coats of paint—two of primer, two of finish, and a coat of water repellant.

Below: The elliptical window on the east end of the Celestial Room is the largest window in the temple. It includes 234 pieces of glass. The frame was manufactured at BDL Mill in Salt Lake City, and Charles Allen did the glazing. The frame alone is 22.5 feet wide, 8.5 feet tall, and weighed approx. 1,000 lbs. The sill was made of redwood planks, glued and clamped together, and the arch was made of sugar pine.

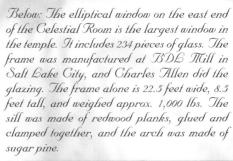

Above: Charles Allen, the designer, builder, and glazier of the temple windows, is an expert in this historical period of window construction. His windows draw light into most of the restored Nauvoo homes on the flats. He creates the windows in his shop just down the street from the temple. As with other building challenges during the reconstruction, the design of the windows had be true to the historic image, while accommodating contemporary use.

S he windows of the temple rivaled the stone as a distinctive feature. In the 1840s, windows were more than ornamentation; they illuminated the interior with shafts of light. Even the shapes of the windows—some round, some with rounding at the top with a half circle—suggested light of a rising or setting sun, or of the sun high in the sky.

Between the two rows of main windows, Joseph Smith asked for a row of round windows. Initially the architect, William Weeks, balked at the variance to accepted practice, but the round windows became a dramatic feature. Above the capitals and between each of the stone stars ran another row of smaller circular windows of painted glass that lit the rooms of the attic story used by the Saints for their special ceremonies.

The varied sizes of the rectangular windows, some with their half-circle top "give the appearance of thrusting up to the stars at the top of the temple," Charles Allen suggests. He knows what he is talking about, having been given the charge to design and craft all 127 windows. He talks of mullions and putty, of moldings and wind tunnels as he describes the process that required him to triple the size of his shop in Nauvoo for this project. Allen uses a historic restoration method that would have been appropriate for the 1840 period, using original mortise and tenon square-peg joinery instead of nails in window sashes and doors.

"I come to the shop every day and look at the windows and just shake my head. I marvel; it's a miracle that the windows came from our shop," states Allen who heads up the family operation.

The glass for the new temple was mouth-blown—as the earlier glass would have been—in France.

Nauvoo Temple

that the windows should be semicircular—that the building was not tall enough to accommodate round windows. Joseph Smith summarily dismissed his objection: "I wish you to carry out my designs. I have seen in vision the splendid appearance of that building illuminated, and will have it built according to the pattern shown me."[11] The round windows became a distinctive architectural feature of the seven-story structure.

"WHEN THE LORD SAID, 'BUILD ME A TEMPLE,' THE MORMONS SAID, 'WELL, YOU HAVE GIVEN US EVERYTHING WE'VE GOT, EVERYTHING WE HAVE COMES FROM YOU, WE'LL GIVE YOU BACK TEN PERCENT.'"

—*Dr. Glen M. Leonard*

JOSEPH FURTHER EXPLAINED that in all ages, the Savior had revealed the pattern for temples. An avid student of the Bible, the Prophet was no doubt familiar with the Lord's precise directives to Moses to prepare a "sanctuary" in the wilderness "according to all that I shew thee, after the pattern of the tabernacle"(Ex. 25:8–8).

Of the planned temple, a reporter for the *Illinois State Register* wrote: "The appearance presented by this edifice in the diagram model, which was shown to me by the Prophet, is grand and imposing. The tower, the casements, the doors, and all the prominent parts of the edifice, are to be richly ornamented, both within and without—but in a style of architecture, which

no Greek, nor Goth, nor Frank, ever dreamed, I will be bound to affirm. Indeed, as I learned from the lips of the Prophet himself—the style of architecture is exclusively his own and must be known, henceforth and forever, I suppose as the Mormon order!"[12]

THE WORK ON THE TEMPLE inched forward at first. The temple quarry on the outskirts of the city was opened October 12, 1840 by Albert P. Rockwood and his assistant Charles Drury. The two supervised the stonecutting for the duration of the project. The solid blocks of limestone from four to six feet thick were roughly cut at the quarry and then dressed and polished at the temple site. Day after day, teams plodded up the hill from the riverfront quarry pulling behind them massive slabs of stone secured to the sturdy timber of a wagon.

"I started with the first load of stone that was hauled for the temple," reported William Allred, "but as I had an ox team, Lorenzo Brown got to the temple ground first as he had a horse team. I worked more or less on the temple until it was nearly done."[13]

WILLIAM ALLRED

Center: Men worked at the limestone quarry just north of the city under the direction of Albert P. Rockwood. By 1844 there were sixty-two laborers with six teams hauling stone to the temple. Stone was underslung on specially built wagons made to haul stone, as well as being placed on traditional wagons.

LUMBER FOR THE TEMPLE came as a result of labor in the pine forests in Wisconsin. From 1841 to 1843, forty-four work crews harvested more than 1.5 million board feet of lumber and 200,000 shingles, which were floated downstream as rafts, usually several hundred feet in length and width. The trip took a week, sometimes two. "Every rapids, every dam, every pier and boom below a mill was a potential danger," recalled Joseph Holbrook.[14] One brother was caught in the whirl in the river above the mills and drowned. When the rafts arrived at the wharf in Nauvoo, large crews of men, assigned by ward, were on hand to move the lumber up to the temple with the help of oxen and horses. The foundation was laid out in February 1841 and workmen immediately began digging. By March, they started the cellar walls, which within weeks were high enough to set the cornerstones.

Opposite: Nauvoo's lumber needs outstripped local resources, so crews were dispatched to harvest wood in the Wisconsin pineries about five hundred miles north of Nauvoo. Workers lashed the milled lumber, logs, and timber into rafts for the journey down the Mississippi. More than 100,000 board feet of lumber made up a raft. Accommodations on the raft were crude shanties and a cook shack. Two men stood at each end of the raft where paddle-like rudders were used for steering. For four years, the teams successfully steered these unwieldy platforms through rapids, currents, and past other river craft, sand bars, and piers to Nauvoo.

AT GENERAL CONFERENCE on April 6, 1841, the eleventh anniversary of the Church, a special cornerstone ceremony at the temple drew crowds of dignitaries, visitors, and local citizens. "Heaven and earth combined to make the scene as glorious as possible," Joseph Fielding reported in the *Times and Seasons*. The newspaper estimated that 10,000 people attended the festivities.

He said of the visitors' experience: "The whole passed off with perfect harmony and good feeling. The people were truly of one heart and mind, no contention or discord, even persons unconnected with the church forgot their prejudices, and for once took pleasure in the society of the Saints, admiring their order and unanimity."[15]

Opposite: Of the significance of the southeast cornerstone of the temple, Brigham Young explained that just as the intense shafts of morning sun in the northern hemisphere come from the southeast, the southeast corner is representative of the most brilliant source of revealed light.

Above: In February 1841 the Temple Committee laid out the foundation; in two months men dug the cellar and placed foundation rock; by April, the walls were ready for laying the cornerstones.

Left: President Gordon B. Hinckley applies the first mortar to the southeast cornerstone of the Nauvoo Temple at a service November 5, 2000. He explained that we are "trying to recreate as nearly as we possibly can that which took place here April 6, 1841." With the President were President Boyd K. Packer, Elder David B. Haight, Elder Alden Porter, Elder Donald L. Staheli, and Bishop H. David Burton. (Also shown in photo: F. Keith Stepan, Managing Director of Temple Construction Department.)

For this occasion, fourteen companies of the Nauvoo Legion bolstered by two Iowa companies of volunteers presented an impressive morning parade. The women of Nauvoo presented Joseph Smith with a national silk flag, and the assembly then moved to the temple grounds.

"This principal cornerstone," announced Joseph Smith, " is . . . now duly laid in honor of the great God . . . and may it there remain until the whole fabric is completed."[16] A student of the Bible, Joseph Smith no doubt drew upon the words of Isaiah—"a stone, a tried stone, a precious cornerstone, a sure foundation" (Isa. 28:16). Brigham Young explained the significance of laying the first stone on the southeast corner, for there shone the first light of day as the sun rises in the east.

One of the guests at Joseph's side was twenty-two-year-old Thomas Coke Sharp, editor of the *Warsaw Signal* newspaper in Warsaw, a community fifteen miles south that saw Nauvoo as a rival for river trade. Fiery and ambitious, Sharp became a bitter foe of the Church and its leaders. Norton Jacobs, assigned to hold Sharp's horse during the ceremonies, said, "I believe [Sharp] here imbibed that spirit of rancor which since has been so freely manifested against the Saints, for he envied that majesty and magnanimity which he had not the honesty and courage to emulate."[17] It wasn't long before Thomas Sharp embarked on a relentless attack: "Whenever they, as a people, step beyond the proper sphere of religious denomination, and become a political

NORTON JACOBS

Opposite: The Nauvoo Legion served important military, ceremonial, social, and symbolic functions for the town. Its regular drills, parades, mock battles, and special activities such as those at the cornerstone ceremonies of the Nauvoo Temple gave the militia a singular presence. Today, mock Legion activities are presented in the historic district. The Nauvoo Legion Benevolent Association banner and Joseph Smith's pistol shown here are found in the collection of the Museum of Church History and Art.

body, as many of our citizens are beginning to apprehend will be the case, then this press stands pledged to take a stand against them."[18]

The day-long event was a day of celebration for the Saints. "Great numbers of people, far and near both Saints and strangers assembled together in Nauvoo," Wandle Mace, carpenter on the temple observed, "to witness the laying of the cornerstones of the temple, which was to be built, wherein the Saints might worship in an acceptable manner before God."[19] Nancy Naomi Alexander Tracy described that in the huge, chief cornerstone, "Brother Joseph had placed a Bible, a Book of Mormon, hymn book, and other church works along with silver money that had been coined in that year. Then a lid was cemented down and the temple was reared on top of this. It made me think of the prophets of ancient days hiding up their records to come forth in some future generation."[20]

WANDLE MACE

To facilitate the scheduling of the work forces at the temple, Nauvoo was divided into sections called wards. They rotated in ten-day shifts. Joseph Smith encouraged the contributors saying, "Remember that he that sows sparingly, shall also reap sparingly, so that if the brethren want a plentiful harvest, they will do well to be at the place of labor in good season in the morning, bringing all necessary tools, according to their occupation, and those who have teams bring them also."[21] The Prophet pledged that those who paid their tithes would be rewarded: "I intend to keep the door at the dedication myself and not a man shall pass who has not paid his bonus."[22]

Offerings in food, clothing, lodging and funds—though they were limited—were accepted as "tithing" as well. The first entry in what was called the Book of the Law of the Lord "was made under the date of December 1, 1841. It was one gold sovereign, valued at $5.00, to the credit of John Sanders, late from Cumberland, on the borders of Scotland, Europe."[23] Most Saints sacrificed to meet their commitments. Zina Huntington's husband Henry sold his coat, vest, and hat "to answer up on his tithing for

$19.50. O may he be enabled to pay his tithing," she wrote in her journal, "that he or we may receive the promised blessings of the Lord."[24]

A small congregation of 27 Saints in the Andover, Ohio, congregation stretched to send contributions. Their sacrifices were carefully identified in a letter with the names of those who donated, along with a note explaining that they hoped to send more later. They contributed twenty dollars in cash, thirteen and a half yards of cloth, a skein of yarn, a quilt, three skins, two pairs of boots and a pair of shoes, some socks and mittens, and twenty-five pounds of apples.[25]

Even the children joined in the effort. "How well I can remember being very pleased when my mother would let me take father's dinner to him while he was working on the Nauvoo Temple," recalled Matilda McClellan Loveless. "I seemed to understand the importance and the holiness

Opposite: This wooden food-service caddy held the women's one-penny-a-week contributions to purchase nails and glass for the Nauvoo Temple. A few paid a year in advance. The women of the LDS branch in Bolton, England, met regularly to support the building project. Their records for June 12, 1843 (shown in photograph) itemized contributions for "the nails and glass for the temple."

To Joseph Smith, the Saints' sacrifice of time, talents, and property was a measure of their love for the cause of truth. Careful records of all contributions were kept. From $194 in donations the Saints funded the building of a new crane to speed the temple's construction. The Saints gave possessions, money, and labor, though Hyrum Smith chided them saying, "We don't want any more old guns and watches."

of the building. Father was always so pleased to have us children come with his dinner and would tell us all about the temple of God he was assisting to build."[26]

Sarah Kimball contributed in a most novel manner. Shortly after the birth of a son, she asked her non-Mormon and well-to-do husband, Hiram, what he considered the child was worth. He paused and she suggested, "One-thousand dollars." He countered that the child, if he lived. would be far more valuable than the sum of one thousand. "One half of him is mine," Sarah clarified. Her husband agreed. She then announced, "Then I have something to help on the temple." She then told the startled father she would turn in her half. Days later, Hiram told the Prophet Joseph of his wife's intent. "I accept all donations," Joseph Smith responded. "And from this day the boy shall stand recorded, *Church property*." He then suggested, "You now have the privilege of paying $500 and retaining possession, or receiving $500 and giving possession." Hiram Kimball deeded property to the Church equal to the $500 donation, much to Sarah's satisfaction.[27]

The Saints sacrificed and worked hard; they hoped for God's blessings; they took seriously their divine charge. Zina Diantha Huntington, like so many who were making a fresh start in Nauvoo, wrote in her journal, "Father bind us as a people together in the bonds of love that we never shall separate. The Temple prospers O Father. Backen the powers of our enemies that we as a people may accomplish thy works, that our soul may be saved."[28]

4

FIRE: ISRAEL'S GOD

*"I believed in the principle of the gathering and felt it my duty to go
although it was a severe trial to me, in my feelings to leave my native
land and the pleasing associations that I had formed there;
but my heart was fixed, I knew in whom I had trusted and with
the fire of Israel's God burning in my bosom, I forsook my home."*[1]
—Jane Robinson

The Mormons' intent was to share their beliefs and vision with the world. Proselyting had been the lifeblood of the faith. The early strength of the Church came from preaching in the Eastern States and Canada. But Joseph, in 1837, described being inspired to spread the message to foreign lands to gather what he called "the house of Israel" to Zion. Missionary efforts began in England, fulfilling what Joseph had received in revelation as the charge to be "special witnesses of the name of Christ in all the world" (D&C 107:23). Many of the early members traced their roots to British soil, including Joseph and his cousin, George A. Smith, descendants of Robert Smith, who had immigrated to the colonies at age fifteen.

In 1840 Joseph Smith dispatched members of the Quorum of the Twelve—his inner core of leadership—to England to preach and gather new converts to Nauvoo. During the previous summer, Joseph had instructed these men in both Church doctrine and leadership to prepare them for their assignment. The men left behind wives and children who were sick, destitute of the necessities of life, and in the care of people as poor as themselves.

"I went to my bed and shook hands with my wife who was then shaking with a chill, having two children laying sick by her side; I embraced her and my children, and bade them farewell," Heber C. Kimball recalled. "It was with difficulty we got into the wagon, and started down

the hill about ten rods; it appeared to me as though my very inmost parts would melt within me at leaving my family . . . in the arms of death. . . . I asked the teamster to stop, and said to Brother Brigham . . . 'Let's rise up and give them a cheer.' We arose and swinging our hats three times over our heads, shouted, 'Hurrah, Hurrah for Israel.'"[2]

In an earlier proselyting blitz to England in 1838, missionaries had found success quickly. With this current venture, these ill and penniless apostles, Brigham Young, Parley P. Pratt, Orson Pratt, George A. Smith, Heber C. Kimball—on his second tour of England in three years—were to join Wilford Woodruff, John Taylor, and Willard Richards who were already preaching to the British people. They went to work quickly.

"We find the people of this land much more ready to receive the gospel than those of America," the missionaries wrote home. "They have not that speculative intelligence, or prejudice or prepossession, or false learning, call it what you please. . . . Consequently we have not to labor with a people month after month to break down their old notions."[3]

The missionaries began publishing the *Millennial Star* to increase exposure to their message. In its first issue they announced their charge: "It has pleased the Almighty to send forth an HOLY ANGEL, to restore the fulness of the gospel with all its attendant blessings,

HURRAH, HURRAH FOR ISRAEL!

to bring together his wandering sheep into one fold, to restore to them 'the faith which was once delivered to the saints,' and to send his servants in these last days, with a special message to all the inhabitants of the earth, in order to prepare all who will hearken for the Second Advent of the Messiah, which is now near at hand."[4]

Meanwhile, efforts to preach "at home" continued; however, the missionaries' message often met with resistance. The *Quincy Whig* charged that the missionary sojourns to England were a last-ditch effort, for "the fire will soon burn out for want of fuel. Already have their conversions become 'few and far between' in this country, and their missionaries are compelled to resort to

Herefordshire, writing to Willard Richards, "I cannot do the work alone. I am called to Baptize 4 or 5 times a day. I want no better man than yourself to connect and labor with me here & help me reep [sic] this mighty harvest."[8]

During the apostles' service in England, nearly 8,000 were baptized. Converts came largely from the working classes—potters, shoemakers, chimney sweeps, brickmakers, carpenters—who had been seeking religious truth when introduced to Mormonism. Missionaries created branches in many of the major towns and cities. In that period, Brigham Young reported the printing of 5,000 copies of the Book of Mormon, 3,000 hymnals, 50,000 tracts, 2,500 copies of the

> *"Mormonism in the 19th century was extraordinarily well organized, almost from the earliest days of the movement. It was evangelical, meaning that it sought converts and eagerly sought to convince other men and women to become Mormons."* —DR. JOHN BUTLER

England and Ireland, among the ignorant and uneducated class, for converts to build up the new Jerusalem, and the Temple."[5]

The missionaries' success in the British Isles was most dramatic, particularly among the middle class whose only hope to advance in society was to leave home and country and begin again. Of the missionary effort the *Birmingham Daily Press* wrote, Mormonism's "promise to lead [English laborers] out from their Egypt of task-work and subjection has made them rally round [the new religion] as around a new Moses sent from God."[6]

Said Brigham Young of the opportunities, "If we could go four ways at a time, we could not fill all the calls we have for preaching."[7] Wilford Woodruff begged for help in

Millennial Star. A system for the orderly emigration of Saints from the British Isles had also been established. The flood of immigrants helped the Church recoup its strength after its flogging in Missouri. Between 1837 and 1846, Mormon missionaries in England baptized almost 18,000 English citizens.[9]

The first organized group of Saints left for America in June 1840. Thirty-two groups of British converts, nearly 5,000, sailed to Nauvoo between 1840 and 1846, paying fifteen pounds apiece for steerage class.[10] Some traveled up the Mississippi; others found their way west to Illinois from the New York harbor. Their arrivals invigorated the efforts to build God's house.

Not every voyage was without incident. "One of the passengers from Preston a woman dangerous ill died," Alexander Neibar recorded

In gathering to Nauvoo, the Saints "bid adieu to their homes and pleasant places of abode" to help build the temple. This work would draw converts to Nauvoo in ships, on foot, by wagon, and in caravan. From 1840 to 1846 a total of 4,733 British saints emigrated to Nauvoo.

The British Saints were cautioned not to go "in haste" or be encumbered with old bedsteads, chairs, tables, stands, drawers, broken boxes, worn-out bedding, soiled clothing, or rusty tools. Vessels were chartered to reduce the cost of passage. Total cost from Liverpool to Nauvoo ranged from 5 to 7 pounds; the route to New Orleans was cheaper than going through New York. All were expected to receive a letter of recommendation from the Church authority before leaving.

In an early voyage, William Clayton led 200 from Liverpool to New York, up the Hudson to the Erie Canal, through the Great Lakes to Chicago, by wagon south to the Rock River, and down the Mississippi to Nauvoo. Francis Moon wrote home, "I know what it is to bid farewell to my native land, but in all these sacrifices and troubles . . . the Lord has helped me and brought me safely through."[1] Another cautioned, "In gathering to this land many shake out by the way, and others after they arrive. . . . Do not persuade any barren souls to come here—we want men of faith who can sacrifice their all for Christ's sake and the Gospel's."[2]

"We did prosper as a people," Joseph Grafton Hovey recorded as converts made their way to Nauvoo. "They did gather from all parts of the world to Zion and they did surely rejoice the things of the kingdom."

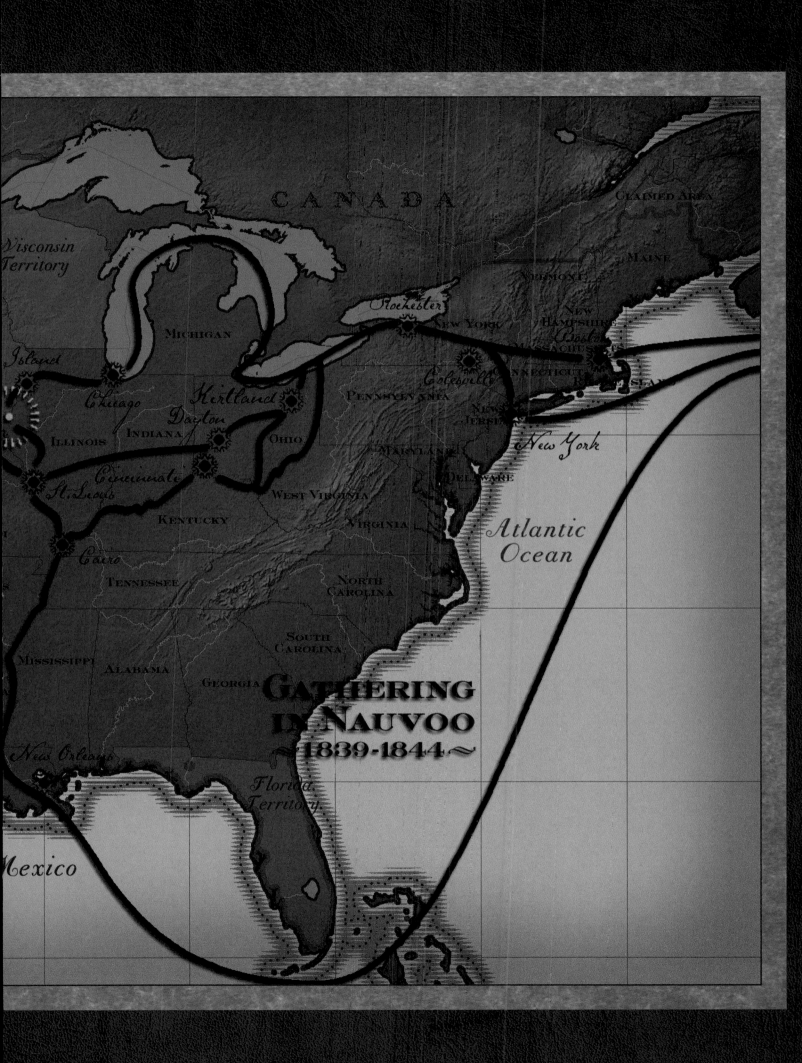

GATHERING
IN NAUVOO
~1839-1844~

of his experience onboard the *Sheffield.* "One of our own company sewed her up in a sheet. Buried about 2 o'clock in the afternoon. Towards 6 o'clock wind ahead blows fresh, increases to a hurricane. Elder H. Clark just making some remarks on the burial of our beloved sister, the ship heaving most tremendously, tubs rolling about pans, kettles and cans all in a uproar, workman shrieking, children crying, all hastening to their beds, wind continuing all night"[13]

Upon arrival in Nauvoo, William Greenwood acknowledged that the emigrants were taken in by the residents. He was hosted by a fellow Saint, "who made us welcome though he was poor."[14] William Clayton, an early British convert to Nauvoo, wrote home encouraging friends and family to join him, saying, "If you will be faithful, you have nothing to fear from the journey, the Lord will take care of his saints."[15]

Some expected Nauvoo, as the centerpiece of the Church, to be an earthly paradise. "Be assured that all who come here must not expect perfection nor a perfect place," wrote John Needham. "If wheat and tares grow together anywhere, it is here; but a day of sifting will come and our trials are only to see what we will bear for the truth."[16] Edwin Bottomly took a lighter approach in his missive home to his father in England, "There is plenty of fruit and fish and fowl but they are the same in this country as in any other, no catch, no eat."[17]

Of the growing congregation in Nauvoo the Prophet Joseph said: "God will gather together all things that are in heaven, and all things that are upon the earth, 'even in one.'" That gathering would include "the elect" of every nation "who hear [the Lord's] voice and harden not their hearts"(D&C 29:7).

Left: Emigration from England was to be organized so that the rich would help the poor, unskilled workers would not overwhelm skilled workers in Nauvoo, and passage across the Atlantic could be accomplished with efficiency and order.

FROM THESE IMMIGRANT RANKS came many craftsmen and artisans, whose work would shape Nauvoo and its temple. William W. Player, a Methodist preacher and Master Stone Mason in Longton, Staffordshire, England, was converted and became a close associate of the apostles. Player presided over a branch of 100 Saints, and when in the Potteries area, the elders often stayed at his home. William and his wife Zillah and their four children—Ann, Zillah, Charles, and William—immigrated to Nauvoo aboard a square-rigger, *The Hanover of Bath,* which left Liverpool March 15, 1842. More than 150 of the passengers were LDS converts. Player's fellow passenger James Palmer described the 5,000-mile voyage by water as "braving the perils of the deep," but found it "a very happy one for those . . . struggling in the same great and glorious cause."[18]

New enthusiasm attended this influx of fresh labor. "Little was done until Brother Wm. W. Player came in June," wrote William Clayton.

Below: Master Stonemason William Player helped construct the notable St. James Chapel, Staffordshire, England, and many stone bridges in the area. As early converts, Player and his family immigrated to America and he went to work on the Nauvoo temple June 8, 1842, superintending the stone work until the last block was set May 24, 1845.

Opposite: Daguerreotype of Nauvoo Temple, one of the few images of the original structure, taken by Louis Rice Chaffin, ca. 1846.

"He was just arrived from England and came with the full intention of working on the Temple." Player's arrival brought much-needed expertise to the pool of inexperienced labor. He had left his imprint on British bridges, canals, "gentleman mansions," and churches, the most notable being the St. James Chapel in Longton, Staffordshire. A spacious Gothic building of white sandstone, the St. James chapel was referred to as "the white church on the hill." Certainly Player's experience prepared him for the significant role he would play in the construction of another religious edifice—on a hill. He went to work June 8, 1842 "and spent some time regulating the stone work already set." By spring, Player had "got all the stone laid round as high as the window sills though the work progressed but slowly having to wait for stone."[19] Player superintended the rock work until the last stone was set, May 24, 1845.

CHARLES LAMBERT

Charles Lambert, a trained stonemason from England, was easily spotted on the work crew—his top hat, suit, and general appearance did not bespeak that of a working man. His commitment was clear: "I worked on the Temple by day, at night was guarding the city; our living was poor. . . . I committed with Brother William Player that I would stick to the temple pay or no pay until finished and did."[20] Miles Romney, converted by the missionaries in 1838 in Preston, emigrated in 1842 to work on the temple. He specialized in circular staircases, and the Nauvoo Temple had two—one on the southwest and another on the northwest. He was foreman of the star builders and carved the capitals for the tower. After the Saints' migration west, Romney later served as the builder of the St. George Temple.

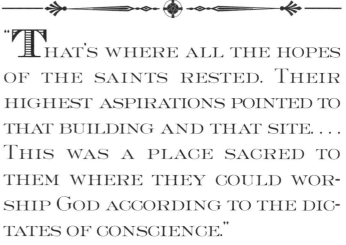

JOSEPH SMITH EXHORTED all the Saints in Nauvoo to give generously of their time and means in building the temple. "The advancement of the cause of God and the building up of Zion," said Joseph, "is as much one man's business as another's. The only difference is, that one is called to fulfill one duty, and another, another duty."[21]

"All who have not paid their tithing, come on and do it," Hyrum Smith stressed as funding fell behind the needs. "We want provisions, money, boards, planks, and anything that is good; we don't want any more old guns or watches."[22]

The women also responded to the call to help build the temple. In 1842 in his Red Brick

"THAT'S WHERE ALL THE HOPES OF THE SAINTS RESTED. THEIR HIGHEST ASPIRATIONS POINTED TO THAT BUILDING AND THAT SITE. . . . THIS WAS A PLACE SACRED TO THEM WHERE THEY COULD WORSHIP GOD ACCORDING TO THE DICTATES OF CONSCIENCE."

—*President Gordon B. Hinckley*

Right: Miles Romney, convert from Preston, England, worked on the two spiral staircases in the Nauvoo Temple, as foreman of the star builders, and as a carver for capitals for the tower. The starstones with the elongated ray at the bottom were referred to by the early Saints as "The Star of the Morning," the brightest object in the sky just before the light at dawn. Also shown are stone fragments from the original Nauvoo Temple.

Store, Joseph Smith established a Female Relief Society whose members were called "not only to relieve the poor but to save souls."[23] Wrote one Relief Society member, "This society had done a great good in relieving the distressed. [W]e have not said, 'be ye warmed and cloathed' without trying to do it.[24]

In June 1843, the sisters expanded their sights that they "might not only relieve the wants of the poor but also cast in [their] mites to assist the brethren in building the Lord's House."[25] Initially the women contributed garden produce and stitched shirts for the workmen; some repaired old clothes while others volunteered to

Above: The Female Relief Society of Nauvoo was organized on March 17, 1842 by Joseph Smith. The sisters originally met to discuss a Ladies' Society but the Prophet expanded their sights, charging them to look to the needs of the poor, to strengthen the virtues of the female community, and to act with charity and compassion.

do washing and donated soap or other materials.

They "cast in their mites" with a penny drive "for the purpose of buying glass and nails for the temple." Mercy Thompson had prayerfully considered how to contribute to the temple and had been prompted by "what seemed to be the whispering of the still, small voice" saying, "try to get the sisters to subscribe one cent per week." She and her sister Mary received the blessing of

Joseph Smith on the effort, and Hyrum Smith added his name to the call for pennies. In a notice placed in the *Millennial Star* in June 1844 the women announced, "We have here entered into a small weekly subscription for the benefit of the Temple Funds. One thousand have already joined it, while many more are expected, by which we trust to help forward the great work very much. The amount is only one cent or a halfpenny per week."[26]

"By strict economy, I obtained the amount," wrote Louisa Barnes Pratt. "I started in good faith to go to the Temple office to bestow my offering. Suddenly a temptation came over me. I conned over in my mind how many things I needed for family use, and that money would relieve my

Nauvoo prospered as no other Mormon community had. In many ways, it was a regular city growing up. Countless farms and fields of grain and produce surrounded the town. The community included sawmills, a flour mill, brick makers, a tool factory, a foundry, dozens of shops selling everything from hats to matches, and plans for a university. Clusters of brick and frame buildings witnessed the coming of age of not only the town but its religion. Situated at a very strategic location at the head of the Des Moines rapids, a substantial obstruction to navigation, Nauvoo was positioned for overland freight handling and passenger business around the rapids when the river was low.

> *"People were attracted to Mormonism because it sought to reshape the nature of Christianity in America which had been bedeviled by a whole series of denominational schisms, divisions, and differences."*
>
> —DR. JOHN BUTLER

present necessities. Then I resisted. Said I, 'If I have no more than a crust of bread each day for a week, I will pay this money into the treasury.' I went forward, paid over the money, and returned, feeling a secret satisfaction."[27]

Mercy Thompson kept a record of all the contributors and notwithstanding the poverty of the people the women collected $1,000. The British sister Saints contributed twenty English pounds to the fund.

The benefit of the Penny Drive was far more than the collection of money. The sisters' sacrifices made a great difference in the building and furthered their commitment to their religion symbolized by the temple. Hyrum Smith, chair of the Temple Building Committee, expressed his appreciation saying, "You sisters shall have a seat in that house. I will stand on the top of that pulpit and proclaim to all what the sisters have done."[28]

However, Nauvoo was not distinguished by its wharfs, mercantile, and trade but by its singular religious emphasis—the temple. Work on the temple took precedence over construction of churches, shops, schools, even homes; yet the project still lagged. During the winter season of 1841 "the work progressed but slowly" wrote William Clayton who posted daily entries of the temple's progress from the small brick office for the recorder, noting that delays were caused by "having but one crane" and "the stone not being cut fast enough."[29] Joseph Smith made it clear what he expected. "[We] have had about three hundred men on the job—the best men in the world. Those that have not complained, I want them to continue with me. And them who hate Mormonism & every thing else that's good, I want them to get their pay & run away."[30]

Joseph encouraged the Saints by saying, "We must, we will go forward; the work of the Lord shall roll forth, the Temple of the Lord be reared."[31] He further encouraged the temple effort by working with his own hands at the quarry and encouraging the people in grand terms: "The Saints seem to be influenced by a kind and indulgent Providence in their dispositions and [blessed] with means to rear the Temple of the Most High God, anxiously looking forth to the completion thereof as an event of the greatest importance to the Church and the world." With confidence he asserted this was truly "a day long to be remembered . . . a day in which the God of heaven has begun to restore the ancient order of His kingdom unto His servants and His people."[32]

The temple would be the most conspicuous public building, the landmark of Nauvoo. Situated dramatically on the hill, it would be seen by anyone coming up the river from the south, down the river from the north, at the bend of the river, or anywhere on the Iowa side.

Joseph Fielding, returning from his mission to Great Britain, was taken by the sight of the temple in the light of the moon. He wrote in his journal, "The idea that it was done at the special command of the Almighty was a new thing in this age. It seemed to fill the mind with solemnity and to give

"NAUVOO WAS DIFFERENT FROM THESE OTHER PLACES BECAUSE IT WAS, REALLY, A UTOPIAN SETTLEMENT. A PLANNED COMMUNITY, YOU MIGHT SAY, WHICH WAS WILLED INTO EXISTENCE BY ITS PRINCIPAL RESIDENT WHO WAS A PROPHET OF GOD."

—Dr. Rodney O. Davis

a sacredness to the whole place."[33] Other missionaries returning from their assignments were likewise amazed at how "extensive had this settlement of the Saints become in so short a time."[34]

However, in the surrounding settlements there were glimmers of suspicion about the new faith and its precepts, and widespread generous concern about its appeal. Some questioned the

"In the Midwest—Ohio, Indiana, Illinois, Missouri, Kansas—the center of the town was the town square and the county courthouse. That was the most impressive building, probably the most expensive building, and people would look to that for their civic liberties. In Nauvoo you have a temple which is a very different kind of a centrality in the civic life of the people of Nauvoo. It is unique and it is remarkable."

—Dr. Edwin S. Gaustad

"foreign" influence taking hold in Hancock County; others simply groused about the growing prowess of a peculiar people, witnessed by their intent to build a temple—while many of them lived in abject circumstances. One visitor expressed concern that Joseph's "mysterious and awful claims to divine inspiration make his voice to believers like the voice of God, trained to sacrifice their individuality; to utter one cry, and to think and act in crowds."[35]

Nauvoo, the people, and the temple signified the unity of faith and community, while other environs were dominated by an adherence to government and its rules. The struggle was ideological; the Saints were on a collision course with their neighbors and their nation. The *New York Sun* stated, "Should the inherent corruption of Mormonism fail to develop . . . sufficiently to convince its followers of their error, where will the thing end? A great military despotism is growing up in the fertile West, increasing faster, in proportion, than the existing population spreading its influence around, and marcelling multitudes under its banner, causing serious alarm to every patriot."[36]

That negative opinion, however, was not shared by other observers of the Nauvoo phenomenon. James Gordon Bennett reported in his New York paper, "The Mormons, under the guidance of their great prophet and seer, the famous Joe Smith, are organizing a religious empire in the far west that will astonish the world in these latter days. Civil, religious, military, judicial, social, moral, advertising, commercial organization, are all embraced within the comprehension of their new system—or their new revelation fresh from God himself. . . . In two years the Holy City of God, Nauvoo, has risen from a few houses to possess 10,000 souls."[37]

Joseph Smith expressed that Nauvoo was both a beginning and an end of his singular mission. "If it should be . . . [the] will of God that I might live to behold that temple completed," he told the people in 1840, "I will say, 'Oh Lord it is enough let thy servant depart in peace.'"[38] He was not granted his petition.

HOLY WORK

"We have received some precious things through the Prophet on the priesthood that would cause your Soul to rejoice. I can not give them to you on paper fore they are not to be written." [1]

— Heber C. Kimball

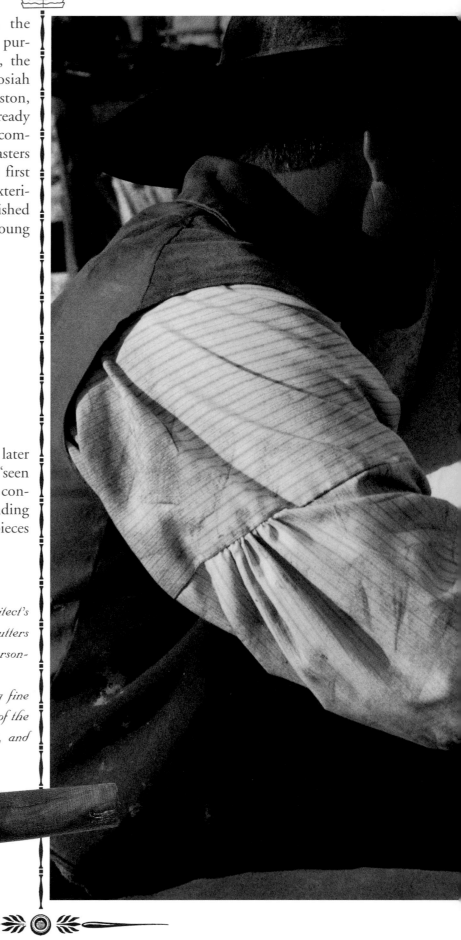

The chiseled stonework on the temple pointed to its sacred purpose. In the spring of 1844, the Prophet Joseph escorted Josiah Quincy, a notable from Boston, Massachusetts, about the already imposing yet nowhere-near-complete structure. While the pilasters were yet to stretch above the first floor, the stone carvings to ornament the exterior were underway. Years later, Quincy published his thoughts about the tour with the young Prophet:

> Near the entrance to the Temple we passed a workman who was laboring upon a huge sun, which he had chiselled from the solid rock. . . . 'General Smith,' said the man, looking up from his task, 'is this like the face you saw in vision?'
>
> 'Very near it,' answered the prophet.[2]

A visitor to Nauvoo from Pittsburgh later described the face on the sunstone as one "seen in old almanacs."[3] Looking at the sunstones conjures up images of mallets, chisels, sanding devices, and ropes to haul the one-ton pieces into place.

Right: The stone carving was evidence of the architect's skill and the ingenuity of the stonecutters. Stonecutters followed an established design, but each left his personal touch on the walls of the temple.

Below: This wooden mallet was used in carving fine detail in the limestone blocks. The stone exterior of the temple features carved images of the sun, moon, and stars as well as simple patterns.

THE CARVED STONES ON THE TEMPLE, the sunstone in particular, have been the focus of much attention over the years. The original architectural features have been reproduced with great care on the new temple. The pilasters, ornamented with carved moonstones at the base and the sun and trumpets on the capitals, stand as dramatic columns around the temple. These dramatic features were more than decoration; they symbolized the signs in the heavens. Joseph Smith saw the prominent stone ornamentations in a vision prior to the temple's construction. He taught that these astronomical symbols indicated the nature of the glorious blessings performed within the temple's walls: "God has made certain decrees which are fixed and immovable; for instance God set the sun, the moon, and the stars in the heavens, and gave them their laws, conditions and bounds, which they cannot pass except by His commandments; they all move in perfect harmony in their sphere and order, and are as lights and wonders, and signs to us."[3]

"It is intended that this temple on earth reproduce a temple plan or model which exists in heaven. So this implies two or three things. First that the temple on earth actually reflect the heavenly sphere in its architecture, namely the presence of the heavenly bodies—stars, sun, moon," explains Dr. John Lundquist. "These are reflected as symbols in the actual architecture of the temple to underlie that this is a meeting place of heaven and earth. Second, all of the great temple-building traditions have had the idea of astronomy, namely that the temple has always been like an observatory."

Of the apparent themes etched in stone, Dr. Richard Ahlborn, curator of the Smithsonian Institute, suggests: "What more powerful statement can you say about a belief in a divine creative power than making reference to what was created." In one of the "largest single acquisitions" by its Board of Regents, the Smithsonian purchased one of the two remaining sunstones for permanent display. Dr. Ahlborn sees "the sunstone as both a material object and visual presence that embodies the values of the people, the culture. The Church of Jesus Christ of Latter-day Saints obviously had, and you can feel it in the sunstone, a presence, a purpose, a sense of what needed to be done and the sunstone tells me all of that."

Dr. Madsen adds his interpretation: "The Saints came to the temple and saw on its exterior the very prophecy of the destiny of righteousness, meaning the fullness of the light of God." The image of stars in the galaxy is captured in the con-

versation between the Lord and Abraham, explains Dr. Madsen. "And the Lord says, 'Look up Abraham.' And he looks up at the night sky and sees the canopy of stars, and the voice of the Lord says, 'Thy posterity shall be like these, they will shine like stars of first magnitude.' So, temple and temple awareness were to fulfill the promises of Abraham in our modern day. That was their faith."

THE SAINTS CAME TO THE TEMPLE AND SAW ON ITS EXTERIOR . . . THE FULLNESS OF THE LIGHT OF GOD.

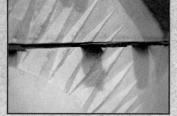

Left: The sunstone is actually two pieces of stone, the face rising above what Brigham Young described as clouds, and two hands each holding a trumpet. The two pieces would have been shimmied into place on the top of the capitals using ropes, pulleys, and a crude crane.

Center: The sunstone is the most recognizable image associated with the Nauvoo Temple. Sitting at the top of the capitals, each of the 30 stones was uniquely carved from Alabama limestone by stone carvers following the same basic pattern. While only fragments of stone from the original Nauvoo Temple remain, two of the thirty original sunstones have been preserved: one at the Smithsonian Museum of American History in Washington, D.C., the other at the LDS Nauvoo Visitors Center.

Left: The five-pointed starstones adorned the top of the pilasters. The elongated ray pointing down to the sunstone suggested that this star, sometimes referred to as the Star of the Morning, drew its light from the sun as it sat below the horizon. Hence, the morning star depicts light as does the Lord Jesus Christ. Next to the starstones are small, round windows that feature a star in colored glass. Stars are often used in the scriptures to represent the endless posterity of Abraham and those faithful to his covenant.

Right: The moon, star, and sunstones were carved for the rebuilt temple by hand as were the original stones. Air hammers and chisels shaped the images; the refinement of these tools made possible enhanced penetration of the stone beyond the nineteenth-century designs, adding increased dimension to the sculpting. Even with sophisticated tools, it took as long as three months to complete just one of the singular sunstone designs. All three designs were cut from Alabama limestone, from a quarry near the one used to supply the limestone for the walls. Shown in photo is Lucien Batalu.

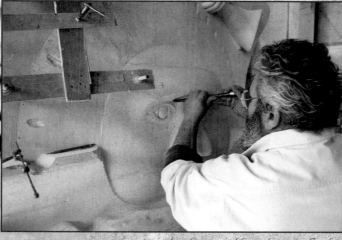

Below: The moonstones, sunstones, and starstones for the present Nauvoo Temple were carved off site in: Salt Lake City, Utah; Idaho Falls, Idaho; Bedford, Indiana; New Castle, Pennsylvania; and Toronto and Owen Sound, Ontario, Canada. They were shipped to Salt Lake City for quality inspection and then on to Nauvoo, Illinois. They were positioned with massive lifts and cranes. In the first construction, a wooden crane lifted the stones into place. When the first capital was put in place in 1844, "the crane gave way which caused considerable danger. By great care the stone was safely landed and set without further incident." Shown in photo is Virgil Badie.

Above: The first moon-stone was placed on the rebuilt Nauvoo Temple on June 21, 2001. Shown above is the stone crew (l to r): Scott Downs (Fore-man), Chris Noe, Luis Torres, Stan Anderson, Larry Martinez, Eric Peter-son, and Steve Christensen (Superintendent). Jeff Franks, a one-year volunteer, not available for photo.

Below: On August 20, 2001 the first sunstone was raised into position on the rebuilt temple and placed on the north side above the third pilaster.

In the 1840s, as many as 75-100 stonecutters were at work in the shop beside the structure. As the structure neared completion, Brigham Young described the configuration of stones:

> There are thirty capitals around the temple, each one composed of five stones, viz., one base stone, one large stone representing the sun rising just above the clouds, the lower part obscured; the third stone represents two hands each holding a trumpet, and the last two stones form a cap over the trumpet stone, and all these form the capital, the average cost of which is

very pleasing and noble appearance, and seem very appropriate in their places.[6]

Completing the ornamentation was a series of five-pointed stars, the center ray pointing down as with the star of Bethlehem. The star pattern was also picked up in the upper round windows in red, white, and blue stained glass. Dr. Loren Horton suggests that "wherever you had the sun, moon, and stars, as on grave markers or other public buildings, it was a symbol of heaven. They were heavenly bodies and where heaven is, God is present. So that reinforces the fact that God's presence is there in the temple."

Just as the rising temple dominated the land-

"THE SUN AND MOON AND STARS WE ARE TAUGHT IN MODERN REVELATION ARE SYMBOLIC OF THE VERY LIGHT OF CHRIST, THAT HE, HIMSELF, IS IN AND OF AND THE CREATOR OF SUCH LIGHT. THE TEMPLE IS A HOUSE OF LIGHT. . . . SO THE SAINTS CAME TO THE TEMPLE AND SAW ON ITS EXTERIOR THE VERY PROPHECY OF THE DESTINY OF RIGHTEOUSNESS, MEANING THE FULLNESS OF THE LIGHT OF GOD."
—*Dr. Truman G. Madsen*

about four hundred and fifty dollars each. These stones are very beautifully cut, especially the face and trumpet stones and are an evidence of great skill in the architect and ingenuity on the part of the stone cutters. They present a

Opposite: These dramatic features carved in stone were more than decoration. They had meaning as Joseph Smith taught: "God has made certain decrees which are fixed and immovable; for instance God set the sun, the moon, and the stars in the heavens, and gave them their laws, conditions and bounds. . . . They all move in perfect harmony in their sphere and order, and are as lights and wonders, and signs to us."[5]

scape, so the doctrines of temple worship dominated the dialogue of Joseph Smith's sermons. The *Times and Seasons* carried regular updates of the building's progress. A January 1844 account records that, "Strenuous efforts are now being made in quarrying, hauling, and hewing stone, to place it in a situation that the walls can go up and the building be enclosed by next fall."[7]

The Prophet Joseph drew from the writings of Isaiah to clarify the temple's purpose in the last days: The Lord's house shall be established . . . and he will teach us of his ways, and we will walk in his paths"(Isa. 2:3). Said Joseph, "The Temple of the Lord is in process of erection here, where the Saints will come to worship the God of their fathers, according to the order of His house and the powers of the Holy Priesthood."[8]

He also taught that by the power of the priesthood, the Saints could perform sacred ordinances, make eternal covenants, and seek the will of the Lord. This power was what had distinguished temple worship in ancient times and had been restored again by God. This is a work he described as "worthy of archangels—a work which will cast into the shade the things which have been heretofore accomplished; a work which kings and prophets and righteous men in former ages have sought, expected, and earnestly desired to see, but died without the sight."⁹ His words were prophetic for he would be martyred before the temple was completed.

Nauvoo resident Daniel H. Wells, not yet baptized a Church member, gave Joseph credit for receiving revelation when he said, "It seemed to me that he advanced principles that neither he nor

"To think that these temples function and we go in there as volunteers to participate on behalf of the dead is the closest we can come to the vicarious act of the Savior who gave his life that we could have life eternal and we give of ourselves for ancestors that we haven't ever met, but we will meet them. And when we meet them we will know their names and they will put their arms around us and thank us."

—ELDER RUSSELL M. NELSON

any other man could have obtained except from the source of all wisdom—the Lord himself."[10]

Early Mormonism drew from a fairly orthodox, committed body of Christians. As a religion it attracted men and women who were accustomed to a church with institutional patterns and doctrines. Joseph taught the Saints of Christ's mission, of His Atonement, of His resurrection, and the hope of the resurrection. Joseph tied temple rites to that hope.

Yet, there were those who turned away from Joseph's teachings, their faith fractured by doctrines tied to the temple. Some of the disenchanted had been Joseph Smith's closest associates. Following a conference of the Saints, William Law, former counselor to the Prophet, said "Some of the most blasphemous doctrines have been taught by J. Smith and others ever heard of."[11]

Unique—and heartening to the members— was the doctrine of baptism for the dead. Early in his ministry Joseph Smith had described the doctrine of baptism as a necessary step to salvation for

all. But it was not until 1840 that he elaborated on the ancient practice described by New Testament apostle Paul: "Else what shall they do which are baptized for the dead, if the dead rise not at all? Why are they then baptized for the dead?"(I Cor. 15:29).

Joseph introduced what he termed "baptism for the dead" in the funeral sermon for a faithful friend, Seymour Brunson. He announced that it had been revealed to him that Saints could be baptized in behalf of their friends and relatives who had departed this life. It is "a privilege to act as an agent, and be baptized for the remission of sins for and in behalf of our dead kindred, who have not heard the Gospel, or the fullness of it," he explained. To those surprised by the promise he spoke plainly, "It is no more incredible that God should *save* the dead, than that he should *raise* the dead."[12] Dr. John Lundquist explains that, "The great temple-building cultures have always had as one part of the temple the inclusion of the dead."

The Saints embraced this doctrine with great fervor. Wilford Woodruff later recalled that Joseph Smith "went into the Mississippi river one Sunday night after meeting, and baptized a hundred. I baptized another hundred. The next man, a few rods from me, baptized another hun-

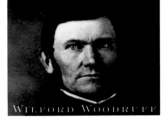

WILFORD WOODRUFF

dred. We were strung up and down the Mississippi, baptizing for our dead."[13]

On January 19, 1841 the Prophet Joseph Smith announced that baptisms for the dead were to be per-formed only in the temple. In a little more than a month, Brigham Young dedicated a temporary font in the unfinished basement of the edifice under construction. Built of tongue-and-groove pine timbers, the oval-shaped laver measured 16 feet long, 12 feet wide, with a basin 4 feet deep resting on 12 carved oxen; stairs approached the laver from either side. A well supplied the basin with water. As the temple neared completion in 1845, the wooden font was replaced with a more substantial one of carved stone.

Elijah Fordham carved the initial oxen for the baptismal font from pine planks glued together. He shaped twelve oxen, four on each side, and two at each end of the font, their heads, shoulders, and forelegs projecting out from under the font. He spent eight months shaping the oxen, as well as ornamental mouldings. It was said that the oxen were patterned after "the most beautiful five-year steer that could be found in the country."[14]

The baptistry proved to be "one of the most striking artificial curiosities in this country," according to a press account. Journalists mar-veled at the size of the laver and detailed the set-ting for their readers. The *New York Spectator* reported on the grandeur of the font:

> In the basement is the font of bap-tism—which, when completed accord-ing to the design, will be a pretty exact imitation of the brazen laver in Solomon's temple. The tank is perhaps eight feet square, resting on the backs of twelve carved oxen. They are of noble dimensions, with large spreading horns,

The BAP

Above: Joseph Smith taught that the baptismal font was to be placed below ground level. For the proxies "to be immersed in the water and come forth out of the water is in the likeness of the resur-rection of the dead in coming forth out of their graves" (D&C 128:12).

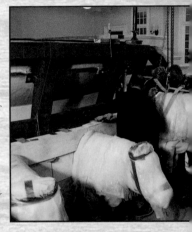

Right: In antiquity, the ox represented the tribe of Joseph, which holds the birthright blessings of ancient Israel and the charge for the salvation of the other eleven tribes. Shown in photo on far right are Ted Orchard and Keith McKay.

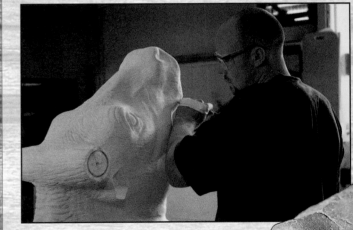

Above: Wade Udall carves the oxen for the new baptismal font out of limestone. His third great-grandfather worked as a stone carver on the original Nauvoo temple.

Right: A fragment of the nose of an original ox in the baptistry of the Nauvoo Temple is one of the few remaining artifacts of those early figures.

Above: Elijah Fordham carved the oxen out of pine planks glued together.

The design of the baptismal font in modern LDS temples is drawn from those in ancient times. Moses placed a font in the courtyard of the Tabernacle, and Solomon enlarged the laver for the temple in Jerusalem, positioning the font on the backs of twelve oxen, each group of three oxen pointing in a different direction as with a compass. The Nauvoo Temple reflects that pattern. The twelve hand-carved oxen were believed to represent the twelve tribes of Israel. The original font was dedicated on 8 November 1841 by Brigham Young. A stone font replaced the wooden laver in the early fall of 1845.

Right: A well near the font supplied the necessary water. Shown is the original drain from under the font.

Far Right: The floor of the original baptistry was made of bricks from the Nauvoo kilns.

> *"In the temple we perform sacred ordinances that relate to the everlasting priesthood. They aren't new. They are revealed anew, but they are as old as mankind."*
>
> —ELDER RUSSELL M. NELSON

represented to be standing in water halfway up to their knees. The execution of the twelve oxen evidence a degree of ingenuity, skill and perseverance that would redound to the reputation of an artist in any community.[15]

Latter-day Saints were anxious to enjoy the blessings of the temple. The font was dedicated November 8, 1841, by Brigham, and within two weeks work for the dead resumed. They later dedicated other parts of the temple as they were finished and then after most of the Saints had left, with the main assembly room still unfinished, they dedicated the whole building and walked away from it.

The significance of baptisms for deceased relatives was not lost on these people who cherished their family ties. Dr. Leonard explains:

> Latter-day Saints came from a small-town, rural culture in New England and the North Atlantic States and even in Europe . . . where every member of the family was part of everyday life, the work-a-day world. Worship centered around the family; life centered around the family. When they lost a family member they grieved. So, for Joseph Smith to say we have priesthood authority that can seal these families, join them together in an eternal relationship that extends beyond this life, it

was an attraction that meant something to them. It not only joined husband and wife and families with children, but the extended family, up and down the generations, and that had appeal.

To Joseph Smith, the temple was a place for worshiping Jesus Christ and learning about the nature of God and man, the purpose of mortality, and the promise of life in eternity. These sacred teachings were included in the ceremony he designated "the endowment." These holy rites, he contended, were the same as those received by the ancient apostles on the day of Pentecost. The Nauvoo Temple had spiritual dimensions that distinguished it from the previous temple of Kirtland. In this new edifice Joseph Smith was promising the people rich blessings that exceeded those witnessed in Kirtland. Here, they would pledge personal fidelity to God; they would secure eternal family ties.

Anticipating his time was short, Joseph couldn't wait for the temple—then not even one story high—to be completed for presentation of the much-anticipated sacred rites and ceremonies. "I have desired to see this temple built," he said to the apostles when they returned from England, "but I shall never see it completed, but you will."[16] On May 4, 1842, he introduced a handful of men including Brigham Young, Hyrum Smith, Heber C. Kimball, and Willard Richards to the ritual ceremonies of the temple. He used the second floor of his Red Brick Store on Water Street for the services.

The upper room of his store was first designed for surplus stock but soon was in use as a special meeting hall. Joseph used the room for

Opposite: In 1840 Joseph Smith expressed his desire that he might live to see the temple completed. He was not granted his petition. He revealed the endowment and sealing ceremonies to members of the Quorum of the Twelve and others in the top floor of his Red Brick Store, beginning in 1842. Photo shows the building in 1890 before it was demolished. It was reconstructed in 1979.

"I don't know what it is, but the Lord bids me to hasten, and give you your endowments before the temple is finished."

ecclesiastical functions, including various priest-hood councils and the organization of the Nauvoo Relief Society. General activities, such as community meetings, theatrical performances, lectures and classes, and debates were also host-ed in that space. But it was the special temple work that gave the setting sacred purpose.

Orson Hyde echoed the urgency expressed by Joseph Smith to carry forward the work of the temple saying, "I don't know what it is, but the

role, "The Prophet told me to assist in carrying water and other commodities to the room above the store. Afterwards I found out it was to give endowments to some of the brethren."[19] These men did not participate in the special services; at the completion of their assigned duties they returned to their homes. They received their endowments about three and a half years later when the Nauvoo Temple was completed.

In later years, Franklin D. Richards spoke

"I REJOICE THAT GOD HAS GIVEN US MEANS WHEREBY WE MAY GET INTELLIGENCE AND INSTRUCTION. IT IS OUR PRIVILEGE TO STAND IN AN ATTITUDE TO GET TESTIMONY FOR OURSELVES—IT IS AS MUCH OUR PRIVILEGE AS THAT OF THE ANCIENT SAINTS. I TELL YOU THERE ARE BLESSINGS [AHEAD] TO BE CONFER'D AS SOON AS OUR HEARTS ARE PREPAR'D TO RECEIVE THEM." —NEWEL K. WHITNEY

Lord bids me to hasten, and give you your endowments before the temple is finished."[17]

Lucius N. Scovil was one of the men who assisted Joseph in preparing the room to repre-sent "the interior of a temple as much as circum-stances would permit." Joseph "told us that the object he had was for us to go to work and fit up that room preparatory to giving endowments to a few Elders."[18] James Henry Rollins said of his

with reverence of the spiritual events in the Red Brick Store: "When the Spirit prompted [Joseph Smith] that his life's work was drawing to a close, and when he saw that his earthly days might be ended before the completion of the temple, he called a chosen few and conferred upon them the ordinances of the holy endowments, so that the divine treasures of his mind might not perish from the world with his death."[20]

Joseph would rely upon those close to him, those to whom he had given the temple teachings, to carry the work forward in the Nauvoo Temple. Joseph Fielding in company with three others received temple rites in December 1843. Said he of the experience, "[In] these things I feel myself blessed and honoured."[21]

Emma Smith, the Prophet's wife, received her endowment 28 September 1843, the first of a small group of women who were endowed by

afterwards gave us a lecture or instructions in regard to the endowment ceremonies." We were led and taught . . . by the prophet himself who explained and enlarged wonderfully upon every point as they passed along the way."[23]

Joseph Smith introduced more than sixty-five Saints to the sacred rites; these men and women went on—without him—to administer the rites in the finished temple. Dr. Truman Madsen describes the endowment as having

the Prophet Joseph. Mercy Fielding Thompson quoted the Prophet as promising that the sacred rites "will bring you out of darkness into marvelous light."[22] Bathsheba W. Smith, wife of George A. Smith, later spoke of the sacred experience, "I received my endowment in the upper room over the Prophet Joseph Smith's store. The endowments were given under the direction of the Prophet Joseph Smith, who

three main parts.

It is first of all like baptism, a making of covenants with God, in the presence of witnesses and as if the Lord Himself was present, witnessing. It secondly is a place of instruction. And in ancient temples it was central to that process, that one understand the entire meaning of creation. So, something to do with the order in which the creation occurred, and why there is even an earth and how it is made, and how we then are to relate to it and to the future. And third, Latter-day Saint temples, which we only have slight glimpses of in ancient temples, were designed for vicarious or proxy service for and in behalf of those who have gone before. And that includes even the covenant of marriage.

Of particular interest was the Prophet's teaching of the uniting of husbands and wives together in marriage—forever. Joseph called it "sealing" and likened this blessing to the promises given to Abraham. With great joy the people embraced the doctrine.

Parley P. Pratt marveled about the "idea of eternal family organization" saying, "the result of our endless union would be an offspring as numerous as the stars of heaven, or the sands of the sea shore." Parley, who had stood by Joseph Smith from the very early days said:

I had loved before, but I knew not why. But now I loved—with a pureness and intensity of elevated, exalted feeling, which would lift my soul from the transitory things of this grovelling sphere and expand it as the ocean. I felt that God was my Heavenly Father indeed; that Jesus was my brother, and that the wife of my bosom was an immortal, eternal companion; a kind ministering angel, given to me as a comfort, and a crown of glory for ever and ever. In short, I could now love with the spirit and with the understanding also. Joseph Smith had merely lifted a corner of the veil and given me a single glance into eternity.[24]

Wandle Mace, foreman of the framers of the temple, wrote of the new revelation: "What a grand and glorious provision for the future, that

"JOSEPH SMITH HAD TAUGHT THEM. IT IS OUR BELIEF WHAT HE RECEIVED CONCERNING THESE ORDINANCES CAME BY REVELATION. HE WAS A PROPHET. HE WAS ACKNOWLEDGED AS A PROPHET. THE PEOPLE LOVED HIM AS A PROPHET. THEY LOOKED TO HIM AS A PROPHET AND THEY LISTENED TO HIM AS A PROPHET. AND THEY GAINED THEIR ACQUAINTANCE OF THESE ORDINANCES THROUGH WHAT HE HAD TAUGHT THEM." —PRESIDENT GORDON B. HINCKLEY

an eternal union can be formed here on earth between a man and his wife, sealed by the authority of Jesus Christ, by men ordained to that power."[25]

In the spring of 1844 Joseph Smith conferred upon the Twelve Apostles all the keys and powers he had received that authorized temple rites. "The Lord is about to lay the burden on your shoulders and let me rest awhile," Joseph announced to his fellow brethren, "and if they kill me, the kingdom of God will roll on, as I have now finished the work which was laid upon me, by committing to you all things for the building up of the kingdom according to the heavenly vision, and the pattern shown me from heaven."[26]

Above: The Nauvoo Temple was the first LDS temple where baptisms were performed for the dead and where the endowment was received by the faithful. The first sacred rites were performed in the temple on 10 December 1845, under the direction of Brigham Young.

Opposite: The First Presidency of The Church of Jesus Christ of Latter-day Saints inspecting a new sunstone.

6
CITIZENRY ON EDGE

"I have good reason to fear that a mob is organizing to come upon this city, and plunder and destroy . . . as well as murder the citizens."[1]

— Joseph Smith

"Nauvoo grew, with magic rapidity, from a few rude homes to a magnificent city," resident Harvey Cluff remembered. "The influx of members of the Church indicated that Nauvoo was destined to be the populous city of the state. Houses increased in number, farms were opened up, and prairie lands east of the city converted into prosperous fields of golden grain. What seemed to give a wonderful effect in thus promoting the rapid growth, was the Nauvoo Temple which was rising in prominence, lifting its white walls above the city."[2]

While progress on the temple gave the Mormons hope, these advances signaled to the surrounding citizenry that the Mormons were permanent. These neighbors wanted nothing more than for the Mormons to leave.

Communities about Hancock County and dissenting factions from the Church bristled as Nauvoo began to dominate not only the bend of the river but the dynamics of the entire county: its elections, its economic initiatives, its military might. Laws outside the boundaries of Nauvoo had little muscle in the Mormon town.

It began as a clash of values. The old citizens of Hancock County voiced the traditional American antipathy for the concentration of power held by Joseph Smith. While Americans, particularly those on the frontier, Jacksonian in nature, were shaping a society defined by pluralism and fierce individualism, the Mormon ethic favored a new hierarchy—a highly connected community founded on the spiritual life.

Politicians and many newspapers characterized the Mormons "as a lawless, infatuated and fanatical people, not governed by the ordinary motives which influence the rest of mankind."[3] Commentary in the *Alton Telegraph* illustrated

the growing tension. "Their religious and political creed are identical, and as directly at variance with the spirit of our institutions as any system that man could possible devise."[4] Thomas Sharp, editor of the *Warsaw Signal,* demanded the Mormons be thrown out of Illinois, saying expulsion would be not only a "measure of wise expediency but one of absolute necessity."[5]

"On the frontier, authority is up for grabs. And here was a group that seemed to define its authority, locate its authority, and even enforce its authority with a leadership that was strong," explains Dr. Edwin S. Gaustad. The liberal charter granted by the state legislature gave the town preeminence as a city-state with full control in the hands of the Mormon hierarchy. This force was both a blessing and a curse. The Mormons built a town from nothing with the temple serving as the crowning statement of their ability, their confidence in God whose people they were. The movement alarmed the old citizens of

Illinois who felt their own way of life threatened.

In an effort to discredit the seeming religious nature of the community, rival religious and political leaders accused the Saints of harboring rogues and joining in illegal activity. Other citizens viewed Nauvoo as a renegade society living by its own rules. John Nevius contended that the Mormons "tell the people that they now come

Below: The view of Nauvoo from across the river showed more than the haphazard development of a typical river town. In October 1844, Brigham Young counseled the people to continue to gather and build the temple as the centerpiece of a stronghold of farms, homes, mills, and industry not "by singing, or praying, or going to meeting, or visiting, or friendly greetings, or conversation, but by the united industry, skill and economy of the whole people."[6]

with the Bible in their hands but ere long they will come with the sword also by their side."[7] They denounced Nauvoo as a haven for criminals and fugitives who seemed to be slipping in and out of the town, some using its religious image as a cover. Hancock County Deputy Sheriff, Joseph A. Kelting, charged, "I have good reason to believe that scoundrels stay in Nauvoo, and when stolen property comes into the city, they are ready to pass it on to the Territory, and screen themselves under the cloak of Mormonism."[8]

> "OUR OPINION IS, THAT EITHER THE OLD CITIZENS OR THE MORMONS MUST LEAVE. THE COUNTRY CANNOT BE QUIETED, UNTIL THE EXPULSION OF ONE OR THE OTHER IS EFFECTED."
>
> —*Thomas Sharp*
> *Editor of the* WARSAW SIGNAL

But the Nauvoo residents countered that their community was more than a conglomerate of homes and farms. Their work—the temple in particular—was "one of no ordinary kind." Joseph Smith had established the town's tone and direction: "Let us realize that we are not to live to ourselves but to God, by so doing the greatest blessings will rest upon us both in time and in eternity."[9]

In this growing atmosphere of hostility, the Mormons didn't rely totally on the Almighty for deliverance. They also mustered the Nauvoo Legion to protect them because of past experi-

ences of being at odds with their neighbors. Commissioned by the state legislature, the Nauvoo Legion was considered one of the largest standing military forces in the nation, charged with protecting the religious enclave. An Illinois newspaper described the force as "a motley crew: some with one pistol; some with two; others with a pike or harpoon; and we even saw some with a brace of horse pistols, a gun and sword."[10]

Outlandish tales circulated of Mormons committing crimes "of the deepest dye" and imprisoning strangers "in a kind of dungeon, underneath the temple," where they were "fed upon bread and water, until death put a period to [their] sufferings." Said one who ventured to Nauvoo in spite of the cautions, "there was not much danger to be apprehended and confined in the subterranean vaults of a dungeon, beneath the Temple." Instead, he calculated that when finished, the temple would "be the glory of Illinois."[11]

The Saints had a few who argued their cause though they gave no endorsement. The Pittsburg *Visitor* maintained that Joseph Smith had "built up a name, a temple and a city, conquering all opposition. . . . We have nothing to do with his doctrines—we only consider him the most remarkable man among the 'diggings.'"[12] An Englishman visiting the Nauvoo Temple in late 1843 called for restraint: "Why disturb the Mormons as long as they are happy and peaceable, and are willing to live so with all men. 'I would say, let them live.'"[13]

But in the end, Mormons found themselves with few allies. Their presence was unsettling to the Illinois towns circling Nauvoo, for their power at the voting booth enabled the Mormons

Opposite: Joseph Smith in an 1887 John Hafen painting of the Prophet as Lieutenant General of the Nauvoo Legion. In his last public address, Joseph charged that the fierce opposition raging about the Saints was moved "by the spirit of the adversary of all righteousness." He called for the Saints to "stand by him," for the mobs sought not only to destroy him, but every one who dared believe the doctrines that God had inspired him to teach.

to make and break political careers and causes. Illinois Governor Thomas Ford stated, "It is indeed unfortunate for the peace that they do not divide in elections, according to their individual preferences or political principles like other people."[14] Even Quincy residents who had just a few years earlier taken the Mormon refugees into their homes joined the furor.

Disagreements between clergymen and congregations in nineteenth-century America were legion. Joseph Smith and his congregation were no different. There were those, some longtime members, who could not abide the Prophet's course. Their intent was to redirect the membership, relying upon teachings that they considered more palatable. Apostle George A. Smith later recalled the Prophet Joseph's response to those who had turned from the Church: "What and who are you? This is the work of God, and if you turn against it and withdraw from it, it will still roll on and you will not be missed."[15]

Joseph Smith had promised that in the temple, husbands and wives would be united—forever—in what he termed "the new and everlasting covenant" of marriage. To this union was tied the concept of plural wives as given to ancient prophets Abraham and Jacob. In private, Joseph had introduced the new teaching to a few brethren

as they returned from missions. Said Brigham Young, "I was not desirous of shrinking from any duty, nor of failing in the least to do as I was commanded, but it was the first time in my life that I had desired the grave."[16] After initial hesitancy, he and others accepted the doctrine as did their wives.

"Like Sarah of old, I had given to my husband [George] five wives: good, virtuous, honorable young women," recalled Bathsheba Smith. "Being proud of my husband and loving him very much, knowing him to be a man of God and believing he would not love them less because he loved me more, I had joy in having a testimony that what I had done was acceptable to my Father in Heaven."[17]

Dr. Madsen explains, "They thought of themselves as lineally tied to Abraham. And that's a tie with temple awareness because Abraham and Sarah are given these sublime promises of priesthood and parenthood and even the likeness of God."

Dr. Rodney Davis contends that "politics in the long run represents the most important source of contention. But the religious aspect, particularly the allegations of polygamy, certainly provided the straw that broke the camel's back."

Hostility was also fed by neighbors feeling estranged from the temple. Outsiders didn't know what was going on in the temple. They feared things they didn't understand. Just as the temple walls divided the world from the secular and the sacred, the doctrines relating to the temple isolated the faithful from those who would leave the fold. There were those who found themselves at odds with the Prophet and his teachings. There are a great many wise men and women in our midst, "who are too wise to be taught," Joseph Smith lamented. "Many seal up the door to heaven by saying, So far God may reveal and I will believe . . . & he who will not have it all will come short of that glory if not of the whole."[18]

The dissidents—William and Wilson Law,

first and only issue attacked land policies, political control, and Church doctrines and officials. Francis Higbee, one of the principals of the enterprise expected trouble: "If [the citizens of Nauvoo] lay their hands upon [the *Expositor* press], or break it, they may date their downfall from that very hour, and in ten days there will not be a Mormon left in Nauvoo."[22]

That trouble came quickly. The paper's first printing would be its last. Eliza R. Snow recorded, "The apostates, aided by our most bitter Gentile enemies abroad, established a press in Nauvoo, and commenced the issue of a periodical entitled *The Expositor*,

"If I'm a farmer in Hancock County, Illinois, I hate them because they work together and they're prosperous and they succeed and I don't have anybody to work with me and I am scrabbling on my little farm all by myself. So, I resent their economic prosperity. I also have a little bit of distrust due to the fact that they have secrets . . . I don't like it and I am going to get rid of them." —Dr. LOREN N. HORTON

William Marks, Charles Foster and others—broke with the Church and took their arguments to the streets. "We verily believe in the sentiment that 'Resistance to tyranny is obedience to God,' Foster wrote to the *Warsaw Signal*, "and with the arms and heart that God has given us, we will fearlessly and faithfully maintain our rights."[19]

John Taylor, the apostle who later led the Church as Brigham Young's successor, answered, "Are a virtuous people to be condemned because they have the moral courage to put a stop to blacklegs, counterfeiters, and the veryest sychophants and snakes that ever poisoned community?"[20] In the ensuing years, the Mormons were accused of committing every crime in Hancock County.

Thomas Sharp encouraged the schism: "We say success to the new undertaking—for a kingdom divided against itself cannot stand."[21] To rally support, these Mormon defectors published a newspaper, the *Nauvoo Expositor*, which in its

in which appeared the most flagrant, scurrilous, libelous articles against the leading authorities of the Church. The mayor, in connection with the city council, declared it a nuisance, and by their order it was demolished."[23]

Opposite: With hopes of giving the beleaguered Latter-day Saints a new start, the state of Illinois granted Nauvoo distinctive legal status with a special charter. The charter granted a standing legion, broad legislative powers, judicial control, as well as the right to open a university. When the tide turned against the Mormons, the NAUVOO EXPOSITOR *declared: "The publishers therefore deem it a sacred duty . . . to advocate through the columns of the* EXPOSITOR *the unconditional repeal of the Nauvoo City Charter . . . to censure and decry gross moral imperfections wherever found . . . to oppose with uncompromising hostility any union of church and state." Officials revoked the charter, leaving the Nauvoo community legally adrift.*

"An Act to incorporate the City of Nauvoo."

Sec. 1. Be it enacted by the people of the
State of Illinois represented in the
General Assembly, That all that
district of country embraced within
the following boundaries; to wit: beginning at the north east corner of
section thirty one in township seven,
north of range eight west of the
fourth principal meridian, in the
county of Hancock, and running
thence west to the north west corner
of said section, thence north to
Mississippi River, thence west to
middle of the main channel of
said river, thence down the middle
of said channel to a point due
west of the south east corner of
fractional section No. twelve, in
township six north of range nine
west of the fourth principal meridian, thence east to the south east
corner of said section twelve, thence
north on the range line between
township six north and range
eight and nine west, to the south
west corner of section six in
township six, north of range eight
west, thence east to the south east
corner of said section, thence north
to the place of beginning, including
the town plats of Commerce and
Nauvoo, shall hereafter be called,
and known by the name of the

State of Illinois
Office of Secretary of State.

I Stephen A. Douglass secretary of
State do hereby certify that the foregoing
is a true and perfect copy of the original
law now on file in my office.

Witness my hand and
Seal of State at Spring-
field this 15th day of
December A.D. 1840.

S.A. Douglass,
Secretary of State.

Right: Following the introduction of moveable type in 1440 by Johannes Gutenburg, printers composed their pages by hand, one metal piece of type at a time. When they finished a printing job, they returned the many pieces of type to their separate bins until the next job. Typesetters were adept at reaching for a piece of type in its tray without even looking.

Above: The presses of the 1830s and 1840s were operated by hand and pages were printed one at a time. An emerging literate population created a deep market for newspapers which were cheap and entertaining. Most burgeoning communities had a small press; the more successful cities had at least a dozen. In 1830 there were 800 newspapers of record in the country, but within a decade, that number had nearly doubled. Many of the small-town publications lasted only a short season because of poor financial backing.

Above Right: In a building on Mulholland Street, the south boundary of the temple, a group of dissidents secured a press and pledged to expose what they considered the evils of Mormonism in a newspaper they called NAUVOO EXPOSITOR. The editor of the WARSAW SIGNAL, Thomas Sharp, encouraged the new paper, saying that now things would develop just as they had hoped.

N WORD

NEWSPAPERS WERE A PRIMARY READING
material in America in the 1840s. The heat of
the dialogue of the nineteenth century—social, political, religious, and literary—prompted the rapid
growth of newspapers which, for the most part, were
provincial, small, and sporadic in publication but far-
reaching in influence. It was considered "the golden
age" of journalism.

The press saw themselves as the champions of
causes, as power brokers, as the last word. They were
often one- or two-man enterprises whose personal inter-
ests drove discussion on the pages. These all-purpose
editors took sides, promoted and provoked controversy,
and generated a body of thought that was, for the most
part, only their own. While the press, in general,
purported to speak in favor of equality, freedom of individual thought and action, and loyalty to the common
good, they took issue with groups that did not fit their
prescribed philosophy. Malicious attacks and one-sided
coverage were common.

Hancock County in the mid-1840s fit the pattern. The LDS-sponsored press in Nauvoo included
the *Times and Seasons* and the *Wasp*, whose stated
purpose was to "convey correct information to the
world and thereby disabuse the public mind as to the
many slanders that are constantly perpetrated against
us."[24] It evolved into the *Nauvoo Neighbor*.

In contrast, the publications in the
areas surrounding Nauvoo—the
Warsaw Signal, the *Quincy Whig*, the
Alton Telegraph and others—took issue
with the Mormon community and its
singular voice. On behalf of their communities they attacked the Mormons,
pointed to the peculiarities of the
one-religion town and mocked what
they considered "high-handed" powers
of the town fathers. Everyone else
stood at odds with most every issue.
That distinction did not stop at
county borders. Newspapers in New
York, Pittsburgh, and Boston were
fascinated by the growing Mormon
stronghold on the edge of the frontier.
And an occasional journalist treated the Latter-day
Saints with a degree of fairness. An article in the *St.
Louis Atlas* in November 1841 commented, "How
long the Latter-day Saints will hold together and
exhibit their present aspect, it is not for us to say. At
this moment they present the appearance of an enterprising, industrious, sober and thrifty population."[25]

"About 6 P.M. a company consisting of some
200 men, armed and equipped with muskets,
swords, pistols, bowie knives, [and] sledge hammers . . . marched to the building and breaking
through the door . . . tumbled the press and
materials into the street and set fire to them,"
Charles Foster later recounted. "We made no
resistance but looked on and felt revenge but
leave it for the public to avenge this
climax of insult and injury."[26]

John Taylor said of the incident,
"The men who got up the press were
constantly engaged in . . . the ruin of
the Saints."[27]

"We hold ourselves at all times in
readiness to cooperate with our fellow
citizens," Sharp announced from the pages
of his *Warsaw Signal*, "to exterminate, utterly
exterminate, the wicked and abominable
Mormon leaders."[28] The Warsaw citizens voted
$1,000 for arms and ammunition, and other
towns followed suit. Across the county, enemies
of the Church readied for war and took up arms.
The Mormons had been threatened with extermination in Missouri, now again in Nauvoo;
once more they were a citizenry on edge.

In an address to a gathering of residents and
the Nauvoo Legion—his last to the faithful—
Joseph Smith spoke plainly: "It is thought by
some that our enemies would be satisfied by my
destruction, but I tell you as soon as they have
shed my blood, they will thirst for the blood of
every man in whose heart dwells a single spark of
the spirit of the fulness of the Gospel. The opposition of these men is moved by the spirit of the
adversary of all righteousness. It is not only to
destroy me, but every man and woman who
dares believe the doctrines that God hath
inspired me to teach to this generation."[29]

In the minds of the locals, attacking Joseph
Smith was the simplest means of ridding themselves of the Mormons. Authorities had for
several years attempted to arrest Joseph Smith on
a series of charges stemming from events in
Missouri. Now, there were new writs. At the
insistence of the governor and with his promise
of protection, Joseph Smith together with his

"There was more satisfaction in Warsaw than any other place when Smith was murdered." —*Dr. Rodney O. Davis*

brother Hyrum and some 30 or 40 others prepared to leave for Carthage. They ascended the hill to the sacred spot—the Temple. A last look at the sacred stone walls marked the young leader's departure from his beloved Nauvoo. He remarked, "This is the loveliest place and the best people under the heavens, little do they know the trials that await them."[30]

Joseph and his handful of loyalists were incarcerated in the prisoners' quarters of the second floor of the Carthage Jail. Carthage Greys, the local militia, unruly and decidedly anti-Mormon, were commissioned to keep the peace. The *Alton Telegraph* described the tension round about: "No one could close his ears against the murmurs that ran throughout the entire community. Little squads could be seen at the taverns, at the tents of the soldiers, and in every part of the town . . . expressions falling from the lips of numbers, there assembled, could leave no other impression upon any sane mind, than that they were determined the Smiths should not escape summary punishment."[31]

Above: Carthage Jail where Joseph Smith and his brother Hyrum were martyred on 27 June 1844. The red sandstone jail in the town of Carthage, the Hancock County seat, was built in 1839 to house petty thieves and debtors, and to temporarily hold violent criminals.

"There was no peace for Mormons and no man punished for murdering them."[32]

—John Pulsipher

Belligerence was exaggerated by Nauvoo's judicial status. Dr. Rodney Davis explains. "By 1844 because Nauvoo had essentially its own court and its judicial system that was separate from the rest of the state, it . . . seemed clear that no non-Mormon was going to be able to get a fair trial in Nauvoo. And by the same token it became pretty obvious that no Mormon was going to get a fair trial outside of Nauvoo. In that respect, the presence of these two competing judicial systems meant essentially that law and order broke down in the county."

Three days later, June 27, 1844, a mob stormed the jail that housed Joseph Smith, his brother Hyrum, and two other Church leaders, John Taylor and Willard Richards. In a swift and calculated attack, Joseph Smith and his brother Hyrum were murdered. The two returned to Nauvoo—in pine coffins.

In the days that followed, the citizens of Hancock County prepared for the Mormons to attack. From Carthage, Apostle Willard Richards sent a clear message to Nauvoo: "I have pledged my word the Mormons will stay at home . . . and no violence will be on their part, and say to my brethren in

Nauvoo, in the name of the Lord, be still, be patient."[33]

While county residents prepared for a Mormon reprisal, the Saints did not respond. Said William Clayton, "It is now left to God to take vengeance in His own way and in His own time."[34]

The assassins and their associates assumed that killing the Prophet Joseph Smith would end the misguided religion and its rule. Dr. Rodney Davis observes: "The citizens of Warsaw wanted Joseph Smith out of the way because they felt that if he were to die then the inhabitants of Nauvoo would become demoralized, the town would disperse, it would collapse, after which Warsaw's economic future would be ensured. The political history of Hancock County thereafter, would be rather more conventionally bi-partisan and the religious landscape would no longer be besmirched by heresy."

Hancock resident Thomas Edmond recorded in his journal, "There is a report that Joe Smith, the Mormon Prophet, and his brother, have been murdered while in jail under the protection of the Governor of the State, by a band of ruffians. . . . Warsaw, Carthage, Augusta and even Hannibal

"MORMONISM DID NOT WITHER AND DIE AT THE DEATH OF JOSEPH SMITH, BECAUSE THE MOVE-MENT WAS ALREADY LARGER THAN THE PROPHET WHO FOUNDED IT. . . . MORMONISM SUCCEEDED BECAUSE IT WAS A MULTI-FACETED MOVEMENT OF EXTRAORDINARY MEN AND WOMEN WHO DESPITE SCHISMS AND DIFFERENCES AMONG THEMSELVES HELD TOGETHER TO SURVIVE THE ASSASSI-NATION OF JOSEPH SMITH IN 1844."

—Dr. John Butler

are in fear and commotion. So much for Mormonism!!!"[35]

The Saints did not retreat to their former homes or cities. They stayed. Their communal grief was nearly unbearable. "Every heart is filled with sorrow, and the very streets of Nauvoo seemed to mourn," wrote Vilate Kimball to her husband Heber.[36] Mary

Alice Cannon Lambert described an anxious city: "I well remember the night of the Prophet's death. The spirit of unrest was upon all, man and animal, in the city of Nauvoo. My father was on guard. No one in the house had slept, the dogs were noisy, and even the chickens were awake. About 3 o'clock the news of the martyrdom was brought to us, and we realized what had kept us awake. And oh, the mourning in the land! The grief felt was beyond expression—men, women and children, we were all stunned by the blow."[37] Said William Hyde, "For a time it seemed that the very Heavens were clad in mourning."[38]

The newspaper *Times and Seasons* took a strong stand: "The idea of the church being disorganized and broken up because of the Prophet and Patriarch being slain, is preposterous. . . . This church fail? No! Times and seasons may change, revolution may succeed revolution, thrones may be cast down, and empires be dissolved, earthquakes may rend the earth from centre to circumference, and mountains may be hurled off of their places, and the mighty ocean be moved from its bed; but amidst the crash of worlds and the crack of matter, truth, eternal truth, must remain unchanged, and those principles which God has revealed to his Saints be unscathed amidst the warring elements, and remain as firm as the throne of Jehovah."[39] They did. The Saints' profound grief was mixed with unswerving determination.

The people followed the directives of the Twelve. Within weeks the work on the temple reclaimed attention. On July 5, a large raft of pine intended for the temple landed at the wharf and crews set to work hauling the material up the hill. Another raft of lumber arrived shortly.

William Clayton recorded that on July 8,

"The laborers resumed their work, although the committee had not so much as a bushel of meal, nor a pound of flour, nor a pound of meat to feed the hands with; but all seemed determined to go to work and trust in God for the means."[40]

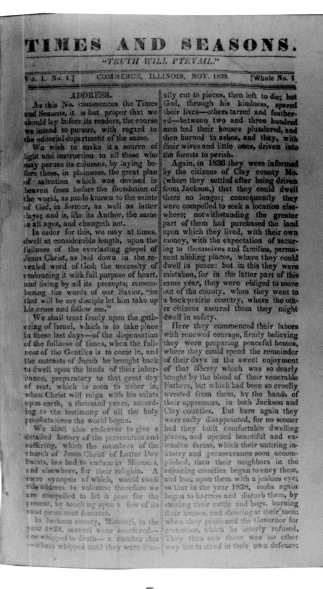

Above: The TIMES AND SEASONS *was the journalistic voice of the Church in Nauvoo from 1839 to 1846. First a monthly and then a biweekly, the newspaper carried Church news; reports and history; doctrinal treatises; world, political, and local news; and obituaries.*

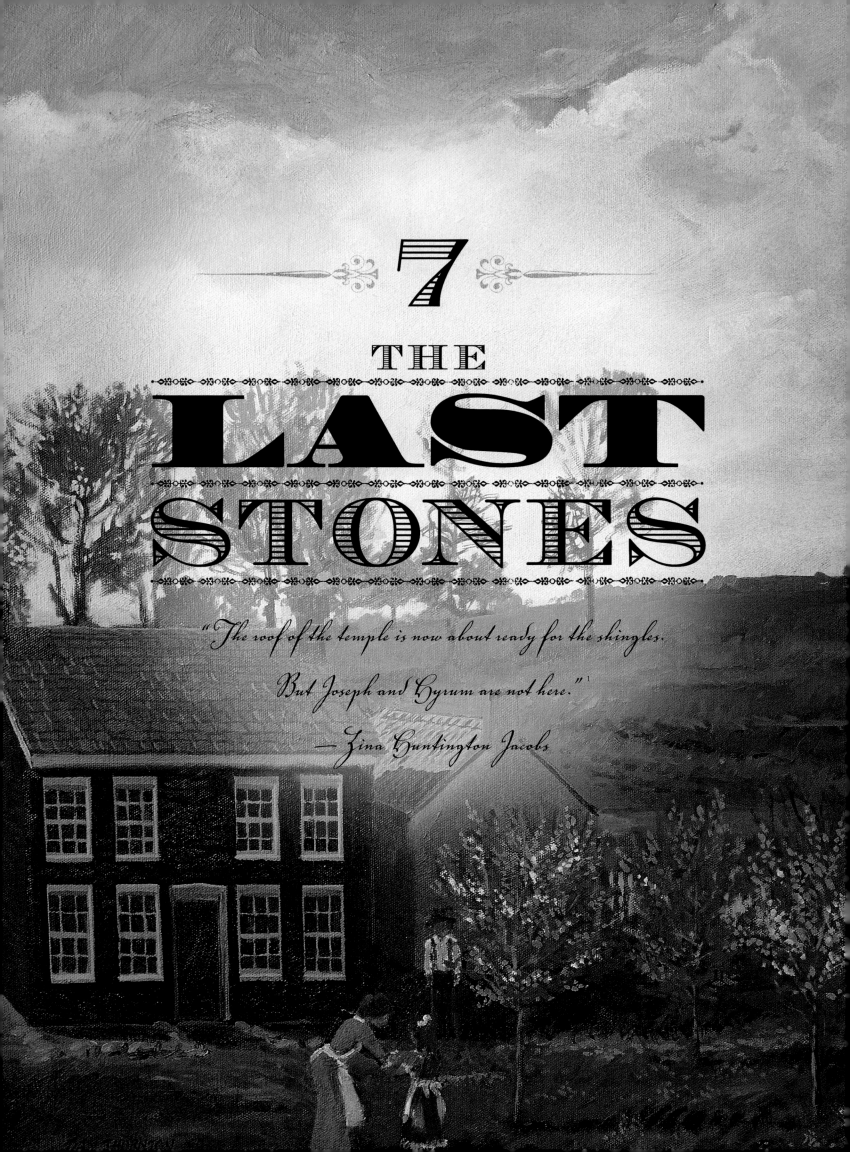

7
THE
LAST
STONES

"The roof of the temple is now about ready for the shingles.

But Joseph and Hyrum are not here."[1]

— Zina Huntington Jacobs

Rocked by the loss of the only prophet the Saints had ever known, the Church struggled but it did not collapse. "We were nearly all wandering in the dark," said Lewis Van Buren.[2] Yet, the faithful did not lose heart. "Mormonism was not dead. Neither was it going to die," wrote Nancy Naomi Alexander Tracy of these desperate times. She, like so many others, had faith that "the Lord could raise up another [prophet] to build on the foundation that was already laid."[3]

Recognizing "a disposition in the sheep to scatter, now the shepherd is taken away," forty-four-year-old Brigham Young, by right of his position as senior member of the Quorum of the Twelve and as one of Joseph's closest confidants, marshaled the support of the badly shaken church.[4] The test of his leadership came in a meeting near the temple August 8, 1844, when Sidney Rigdon entreated the people to follow him. A Church officer from the early days in Kirtland, Rigdon had distanced himself from and even denounced Joseph Smith. Brigham Young responded, "Brother Joseph, the prophet, has laid the foundation for a great work and we will build upon it. . . . There is an almighty foundation laid, and we can build a kingdom such as there never was in this world. . . . "[5] His words stirred the members; but it was his countenance that solidified his position at the head of the Church.

"If I had not seen him with my own eyes, there is no one that could have convinced me that it was not Joseph Smith,"[6] wrote Apostle Wilford Woodruff. "Brother Brigham looked and talked so much like Joseph that for a minute we thought it was Joseph," eight-year-old Mary Field reported.[7] "The likeness was so marked," said Robert Taylor Burton, "that I could hardly make myself believe that the Prophet had not himself returned."[8] George Morris recorded, "I was startled by hearing Joseph's Voice. He had a way of clearing his throat before he began to speak—by a peculiar Effort of His own—like Ah-hem—I raised my Head suddenly—and the first thing I saw was Joseph—as plain as I ever saw Him in my life. . . . That was Testimony enough to convince me where the Proper authority rested."[9]

Rigdon, however, did not go quietly. He announced that without his leadership not another stone would be raised upon the walls of the temple. Determined to prove him wrong,

> "**I** INQUIRED OF THE LORD WHETHER WE SHOULD STAY HERE AND FINISH THE TEMPLE. THE ANSWER WAS WE SHOULD. . . . I HAVE TO WALK [AS IF] JOSEPH IS RIGHT WITH ME ALL THE TIME—ALL I DO TO BUILD UP THE KINGDOM IS JUST AS IF JOSEPH WAS LOOKING ME RIGHT IN THE EYE—AND OUR HEARTS AND FEELINGS ARE ONE."
>
> —*Brigham Young*

William Player and two others went straight to the temple site and "raised and set a stone upon the wall making this prediction a failure."[10]

In the next few years, several others—Lyman Wight, James J. Strang, George Miller—contended for leadership of the more than thirty thousand members scattered from Nauvoo to Canada, from the East and across the Atlantic to England. But their efforts to wrest the core of the Church from Brigham Young and the Quorum of the Twelve floundered. The majority of the Saints turned to Brigham, President of the Quorum of the Twelve, and the Apostles. Said William W. Phelps: "We have hitherto walked by sight. If any man wanted to know anything, he had only to go to Brother Joseph. Joseph is gone, but he has not left us comfortless. If you want to do right, uphold the Twelve."[11] Arza Adams, who had carried the news of the martyrdom of Joseph and Hyrum to Nauvoo, expressed the resolve of the Saints: "Brigham Young on whom the mantle of the prophet Joseph has fallen is a man of God."[12]

Dr. Edwin S. Gaustad notes, "Mormonism could very easily have unraveled when Joseph Smith was assassinated because there were voices, many choirs of doom, many choirs of 'follow me.' Brigham Young's voice eventually became the strongest voice."

The fate of the Saints, the Church, and the temple lay in Brigham's hands. "I inquired of the Lord whether we should stay here and finish the Temple," Brigham explained. "The answer was we should."[13] Brigham later commented, "I have to walk [as if] Joseph is right with me all the time—all I do to build up the Kingdom is just as if Joseph was looking me right in the eye—& our hearts & feelings are one."[14]

"Brigham Young wanted to complete Joseph's dream," President Gordon B. Hinckley states. Expecting the mobs to come again, Brother

"WE HAVE HITHERTO WALKED BY SIGHT. IF ANY MAN WANTED TO KNOW ANYTHING, HE HAD ONLY TO GO TO BROTHER JOSEPH. JOSEPH IS GONE, BUT HE HAS NOT LEFT US COMFORTLESS. IF YOU WANT TO DO RIGHT, UPHOLD THE TWELVE."

—*William W. Phelps*

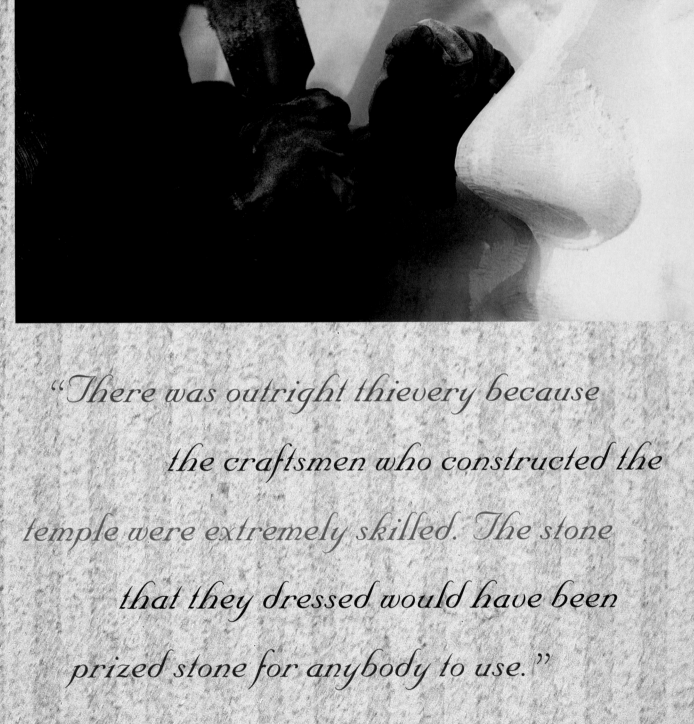

"There was outright thievery because

the craftsmen who constructed the

temple were extremely skilled. The stone

that they dressed would have been

prized stone for anybody to use."

—Dr. Loren N. Horton

Brigham, as they came to call him, mobilized the people to get the temple finished. He posted guards to protect the structure, in particular the stone. "There was outright thievery because the craftsmen who constructed the temple were extremely skilled," claims Dr. Loren Horton. "The stone that they dressed would have been prized stone for anybody to use for building purposes. So, it would be no accident that somebody would come and try to take some of it."

In the next eighteen months, progress on the temple exceeded that of the previous three years. In March 1845, President Young called for four hundred additional men to work on the temple; the following day 105 showed up for work with 30 teams in response to his request.[15] "We hear the laborers sing and shout as they raise the timbers,"[16] wrote Irene Hascall.

Nancy Tracy who lived near the temple described a similar scene: "Out of my bedroom window I could see the masons at work and could hear the click of their hammers and hear their sailor songs as they pulled the rock in place with pulleys. It was grand to see."[17] Joseph Grafton Hovey described, "[I] cut one star and its base and also one window and capts and clousures on the temple building. . . . I do not spend my time heedlessly but labor with all my might on the Lord's House cutting stone to beautify his Temple."[18]

It was a season, said Church authorities in a letter to their brethren in England, of "perfect peace."[19] But the peace was short-lived.

Before his death, Joseph Smith and the Twelve Apostles had discussed relocating in the west and had even organized scouting parties though persecution kept them at home. In the winter of 1845 the Church leadership examined maps with attention to selecting a location west of the Rocky Mountains for the Saints. They read various works written by travelers in those regions. They hoped to finish the temple in time to make adequate preparations for an orderly removal.

They were being pushed to move—and soon—by the governor and others. Soon. Governor Thomas Ford wrote Brigham Young, "Your religion is new, and it surprises the people

as any great novelty in religion generally does. They cannot rise above the prejudices excited by such novelty. If you get off by yourselves you may enjoy peace; but surrounded by such neighborhood I confess I do not foresee the time when you will be permitted to enjoy quiet."[20]

Manpower for work on the temple was plentiful; cash was not. The Saints donated what they could spare—and more. Still the coffers were slim. "It was difficult to get bread and other provisions for the workmen to eat," Brigham Young

"IF YOU GET OFF BY YOUR-SELVES YOU MAY ENJOY PEACE, BUT SURROUNDED BY SUCH NEIGHBORS I CONFESS I DO NOT FORESEE THE TIME WHEN YOU WILL BE PERMIT-TED TO ENJOY THE QUIET."

—Governor Thomas Ford

recalled. "I counseled the committee who had charge of the temple funds to deal out all the flour they had, and God would give them more; and they did so; and it was but a short time before Brother Toronto came and brought me twenty-five hundred dollars in gold. . . . So I opened the mouth of the bag and took hold at the bottom end, and gave it a jerk towards the bishop, and strewed the gold across the room and said, now go and buy flour for the workmen on the temple and do not distrust the Lord any more; for we will have what we need."[21]

By September 1844 the first of the sun stones—weighing about two tons—was lifted into place. William Clayton recorded: "As the brethren were beginning to raise one of the capitals, having neglected to fasten the guys, the crane fell over with a tremendous crash, breaking it considerably. As soon as it was perceived that the crane was falling, the hands fled to get

the five-year building project—Moses Horn in a blasting accident at the quarry, and Elijah Cunningham drowned at the Wisconsin Pineries.

"Great numbers of carpenters, masons, and other workmen are daily engaged in this arduous undertaking," John Taylor reported, "so that not only is stone being prepared, but the sash, flooring, seats, and other things are pro-

Below: The temple was a fascination to the Mississippi River tourist traffic. By 1844 a handful of steamboats a day stopped at Nauvoo. Visitors marveled at the magnificent structure and its strategic location.

out of the way. One of the brethren, Thomas Jaap, running directly in the course of the falling crane, barely escaped being killed. The crane struck the ground and was within a foot of striking his head. This circumstance hindered the workmen some; but in a few days the crane was mended, reared and the brethren again went to work on it."[22] The work was not without incident; however, only two deaths were reported in

gressing rapidly, so to rush the work forward." Plans were, Taylor said, "to commence giving the endowments next fall."[23]

Three months later, December 6, 1844, the last of these huge sunstones was hoisted up amid cheers and congratulations. "It seemed as though the Lord held up the weather until this important piece of work was accomplished," William Clayton recorded. "About two hours after the

"IT SEEMED AS THOUGH THE LORD HELD UP THE WEATHER UNTIL THIS IMPORTANT PIECE OF WORK WAS ACCOMPLISHED. ABOUT TWO HOURS AFTER THE CAPITAL WAS SET IT COMMENCED SNOWING VERY BRISKLY . . . THERE WERE THEN TWELVE OF THE CAPITALS WITHOUT THE TRUMPET STONES; AND THEY REMAINED IN THIS STATE UNTIL THE FOLLOWING SPRING."

—*William Clayton*

capital was set it commenced snowing very briskly, and at night the ground was covered about four inches, and it froze very keenly. There were then twelve of the capitals without the trumpet stones; and they remained in this state until the following Spring."[24]

As the weather warmed, William Player and his crew finished securing the trumpet stones and then began setting the starstones, the first being placed on the southeast corner where Joseph Smith had laid the temple cornerstone. Brigham Young selected a room on the southeast for his office, explaining, "There is the most light."[25] The southeast corner of the temple received the most intense light of the sun and that brilliance symbolized the strongest source of light—the Son of God.

"The temple is indeed a noble structure, and I suppose the architects of our day know not of what order to call it. Gothic, Doric, Corinthian or what. I call it heavenly," wrote Joseph Fielding in his journal.[26]

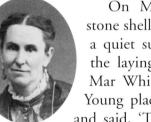

On May 24, 1845, with the stone shell of the temple completed, a quiet sunrise ceremony heralded the laying of the capstone. Helen Mar Whitney reported, "President Young placed the stone in position and said, 'The last stone is now laid upon the temple, and I pray the Almighty, in the name of Jesus, to defend us in this place, and sustain us until the temple is finished and we have all got our endowments.' . . . The scene was a very impressive one and we doubt not that the angels looked upon it and rejoiced."[27]

President Young gave the laborers a holiday and called for the crowd to give thanks to God that they completed the exterior and to pray that the interior would be finished by year's end. He then led the crowd in the "Hosanna Shout." The women waved white handkerchiefs in the morning sky, the men their hats in tribute to the great accomplishment. A band of mobbers stood a distance from the crowd but did not advance. Brigham Young concluded the services with "So let it be, Lord Almighty."[28] Wrote George A. Smith of his feelings, "I could not suppress a flood of tears. My father and hundreds of others wept. We dismissed the assembly as the mob had gathered in town with writs of attachments for some of the twelve."[29]

Things really didn't begin to become critical as far as the continued existence of the city until a year or so after the death of Joseph Smith. It wasn't the temple itself that provoked the Nauvoo neighbors; it was that the building signified permanence, retrenchment, and a measure of accomplishment beyond that of any other locality. "The Mormons will never leave Nauvoo. They would relinquish life as soon as they would voluntarily, en masse, leave their glorious habitation, which to them is the gate of

"BRIGHAM YOUNG WAS A SUPERB INSTITUTIONAL LEADER. HE WAS A SUPERB POLITICIAN AND HE WAS A PROPHET WHO CONTINUED IN SMITH'S VEIN BUT DID NOT UPEND SMITH'S PRINCIPAL TEACHINGS."

—Dr. John Butler

heaven,"[30] judged the *New York Spectator*. All the more reason, in the eyes of the agitators, to drive the Saints from the state.

Norton Jacobs, a steady hand at the temple, recalled, "Brother Joseph Smith said some two years ago about the time the temple was finished, 'all hell would be raised.'" Norton's assessment was that Joseph had prophesied well. "The spirit of the people was raised to boiling heat."[31] The workers slept within the walls with their rifles at their heads at night.

The Illinois citizenry intensified their efforts to force either a collapse of the religion or an exodus of the adherents. The *Warsaw Signal* pages routinely carried threats; this one from William P. Richards: "The probability is [the Mormons] present rampant religious zeal would evaporate in a single generation and the sect as such, become extinct; whilst if they remain where they are, it is certain that this entire generation will witness constant turmoil, collision, outrage and perchance—extensive bloodshed . . . can anyone be sure that they can be got rid of forever?"[32]

"Got rid of" . . . "bloodshed" . . . the Mormons had heard those words before. They knew what was coming. "This morning we received information from Lima, that the mobs were burning houses there," John Taylor recorded in his journal. "The Twelve held a council and thought it advisable as we're going west in the spring to keep all things quiet."[33]

"It's not uncommon to find harsh, physical violence—death, bombings, murder, beatings and burnings of homes, buildings, churches, farms," Dr. John Butler contends. "This was a commonplace phenomena in nineteenth-century America, not everywhere, but common enough that Americans knew how to practice this kind of violence and they were good at it. And that cost Joseph Smith his life, and it cost many Mormons their homes, their farms, their livelihoods."

"Conditions in Hancock County bordered on civil war," recalled George A. Smith of the perilous times. "The persecution was blazing on every hand, and the reputable authorities 'could do nothing for us;' which was equal to saying, 'Hold on, and let us run our daggers into you.'"[34]

"YOU HAVE A LOT OF HOSTILITY AND OUTRIGHT VIOLENCE FROM THE GENTILE NEIGHBORS. PERHAPS NOT DIRECTLY TRYING TO KEEP THEM FROM FINISHING THE TEMPLE, BUT JUST GENERALLY CAUSING TROUBLE. AND THERE WAS THIEVERY AND ATTEMPTED ARSON AND THINGS LIKE THAT. IT WAS GENERALLY TO TRY TO . . . ON ONE HAND TO HURRY THEM . . . AND ON THE OTHER HAND IF THE TEMPLE IS THIS IMPORTANT, THEN WE WANT TO INTERRUPT THE BUILDING OF IT BECAUSE THAT WILL BE BAD FOR THEM."

—*Dr. Loren N. Horton*

Apostle Willard Richards added his voice to the growing tumult: "We assure the governor, if he can manage human butchers, he has nothing to fear from *harmless*, timid, and law abiding Latter-day Saints."[35]

"There is much to be done," said Brigham as he pushed the work on the temple forward, assuring the laborers, "You have men among you who sleep with one eye open."[36] Laborers spoke of working days in the temple with a rifle hid in the shavings, hid because Nauvoo was teaming with spies and false brethren. One man described, "planing up boards and laying floors in the attic and tower. After this I went to work on the arsenal."[37]

The tension was not lost on the children. "I can remember my father coming home in the night (having been on guard) to make bullets in our fireplace," wrote Matilda Loveless. "We were always in dread of the mobs. Father occasionally wore a red coat and we children spoke of father as belonging to the red coat company."[38]

In the fall, several hundred vigilantes met in Carthage and demanded that Nauvoo residents be forced from the state. "The war clouds began to gather around," recalled George

> *"We assure the governor, if he can manage human butchers, he has nothing to fear from harmless, timid, and law abiding Latter-day Saints."* —WILLARD RICHARDS

Whitaker, threatening to "drive the Latter-day Saints from Nauvoo. . . . Business was paralyzed, excepting the work on the Temple, which was going on very rapidly."[39] The mob grew bolder, attacking outlying settlements, threatening women and children, burning homes and crops. In droves, the outlying residents poured into Nauvoo for shelter; they had only what they could carry. Wrote one young mother, "Our house was filled."[40]

Church officers offered prayers that the Lord would give them "wisdom to manage affairs with the mob"[41] and "that the Lord would enable [them] to finish the temple . . . and obtain their endowments."[42]

Above: Stacey A. Dickerson of the Verdin Company (which specializes in bells, carillons, and clocks) adjusts the hands on one of the four aluminum clocks on the tower—each of which measures six feet in diameter.

The clock hands were custom designed to replicate the original architectural drawings by William Weeks. The minute hand measures three feet from center to tip, and the hour hand measures two feet. The clocks are painted in "Nauvoo White."

Above: The temple bell was hoisted to the temple tower July 3, 2001. It was custom made by a Cincinnati, Ohio, firm and cast in a foundry in the Netherlands. It bears the date of its casting, 2001, as well as the date of the temple's completion, 2002. At 33 inches in diameter, the bronze-alloy bell weighs 846 pounds. The bell, which hangs about nine feet below the sixteen-foot ceiling, is protected by fixed louvers that will allow air to circulate while providing shelter from the weather.

Left: True to the design of the original temple, the tower houses a bell and four clocks, one on each of its sides. Integrated with the computerized clocks, the bell has an electronically driven striker and is pitched to sound a near F sharp on the music scale.

GLORY

JOSEPH SMITH PROPOSED in July of 1840, before construction of the temple had even begun, that atop the Nauvoo Temple would stand "a great and high watch tower and in the top thereof we will suspend a tremendous bell that when it is rung shall rouse the inhabitants of Madison, wake up the people of Warsaw, and sound in the ears of men [in] Carthage."[43]

In August of 1845 that tower was finished and "all hands partook of a feast of melons" in celebration. That winter, January 30, 1846, the weather vane was secured to the tower top. A glittering angel is described by numerous accounts much like that of Thomas Kane who referred to the "angel and trumpet on the summit of its lofty spire." The tower and spire faced west and were visible from a distance of twenty miles. Wilford Woodruff claimed the tower pointed "towards heaven, in honour of the united efforts of the Saints."[44]

Once completed, the temple tower was a favorite lookout for Nauvoo residents who climbed the many winding stairs to the lofty perch. A New York reporter wrote, "The view from the top of the temple is majestic and highly picturesque. One can see the large rolling prairies to the east interspersed with growth of trees. One can look down upon the rising city of Nauvoo across the mighty Mississippi to the West."[45] At one point, the Nauvoo band positioned themselves on the completed tower to entertain the congregation in the grove below. In the September 1846 Battle of Nauvoo, the bell tower porch of the temple served as an ideal lookout from which to view the skirmishes.

Inside the tower hung a bell contributed by the British Saints. Brigham Young suggested that they furnish the bell for the temple; and Wilford Woodruff, then in England, put out an appeal "to the hearts and minds of some ten thousand" to bring their tithes and offerings sufficient to purchase a bell for the House of God. A clock for the temple was added to their efforts. The Nauvoo Temple bell was cast in bronze in England and brought by Wilford Woodruff to Nauvoo.

THEY WERE GETTING CLOSE. "The framework of the roof is on the building, and the next week the brethren expect to put on the shingles; the framework around the foundation of the tower is all up, and the first timbers for the tower itself were raised this day. The new stone font is mostly cut," wrote Brigham Young to the missionaries serving in England. "We expect in about five or six weeks the attic story of the temple and the font will be finished and ready for dedication, and just as soon as they are ready we shall dedicate them. We have all the timbers for the Temple on the ground, and above one hundred thousand shingles for the roof. The lead for the eaves and the tin for the dome of the tower are also bought . . . most of the woodwork for the Temple is finished, all the window frames and sashes are made, and the glaziers are ready to set the glass, which we expect here in a few days, the frame and ornamental work of the tower is all ready to be put up, and the whole is far on the way of completion."[46]

Brigham was resolute: "I would rather pay out every cent I have to build up this place and get an endowment, if I were driven the next minute without anything to take with me."[47] His words proved to be prophetic.

A formal dedication was planned for April 1846. But with heightened hostilities, plans changed abruptly. Groups of citizens in Carthage and Warsaw had been behind strikes on the settlements but when once-friendly residents in Quincy turned on the Mormons, exodus was imminent. The *Quincy Whig* reported, "It is a settled thing, that the public sentiment of the state is against the Mormons, and it will be in vain for them to contend against it."[48] The membership of the Church voted to leave in the spring "when grass grows and water runs"[49] and "would then remove to a place so remote that there would be no danger of any more collisions."[50]

 ork was drawing to a close. "The blessing of God has attended the whole progress of the work. . . . Our enemies have threatened all the time," William Clayton wrote. "But the saints have invariably pursued a steady course of work."[51]

By October 5, the Temple was sufficiently completed to host the first general conference, the first in three years. "In the midst of trials, tribulations, poverty, and worldly obstacles—solemnized in some instances by death—about five thousand Saints had the inexpressible joy and great gratification to meet for the first time in the House of the Lord in the City of Joseph,"[52] said President Young. At this conference, Brigham and the Twelve presented a plan to move west.

"THE DAY WAS OCCUPIED MOST AGREEABLY IN HEARING INSTRUCTIONS AND TEACHINGS, AND OFFERING UP THE GRATITUDE OF HONEST HEARTS, FOR SO GREAT A PRIVILEGE, AS WORSHIPING GOD WITHIN, INSTEAD OF WITHOUT, AN EDIFICE, WHOSE BEAUTY AND WORKMANSHIP WILL COMPARE WITH ANY HOUSE OF WORSHIP IN AMERICA, AND WHOSE MOTTO IS: 'HOLINESS TO THE LORD.'" —*Brigham Young*

"From mites and tithing, millions had risen up to the glory of God, as a Temple, where the children of the last kingdom could come together and praise the Lord," said President Young in a dedication of the yet-to-be-completed structure. "I opened the services of the day by a dedicatory prayer, presenting the Temple, thus far completed, as a monument of the saints' liberality, fidelity, and faith concluding, 'Lord, we dedicate this house and ourselves, to thee.'"[53]

"We were told that the spirit of the mob was so bitter against us that we would have to leave the confines of civilization and go beyond the Rocky Mountains," George Whitaker reported. The people were counseled "to go to work and finish the temple according to the revelation given to Joseph Smith, so that we might receive our washings and anointings and the keys and

Below: The Nauvoo Temple stood in stark contrast to the raw-boned frontier of the Mississippi River valley. Joseph Smith had placed it facing west—perhaps as a sign of the forced mass exodus ahead.

powers of the Holy Priesthood, and also the Holy Anointings and Sealings that the power of God might rest upon His servants."[54]

"It was voted unanimously to move en masse from the United States to some place where we could live in peace," Warren Foote reported. "Some place in the west, we knew not where, neither did we much care, so that we could get out of the reach of the mob-bers."[55] That evening following the service, the Nauvoo police force rolled a cannon into place on the north side of the temple. For protection.

State action had contributed to the embattled state of the Mormons. The Illinois legislature

move as "a new epoch, not only in the history of the church, but of this nation." He concluded, "Wake up, wake up, dear brethren . . . to the present glorious emergency in which the God of heaven has placed you to prove your faith by your works, preparatory to a rich endowment in the Temple of the Lord, and the obtaining of promises and deliverances, and glories for your-selves and your children and your dead."[56]

The question asked most often by historians of the period is: "Why would they finish the temple knowing that they were going to leave it?" Dr. Loren Horton suggests. "The answer is in their religious faith. They needed the temple for what was going to be done for them in the

"The thing that held the Mormon community together was its religion. It was not a political community, an economic community; it was a religious community. And any group that is persecuted tends, if they survive the persecution, to be much more closely knit, much more steadfast in their devotion and in their commitment. And that certainly proved to be the case here."

—Dr. Edwin S. Gaustad

revoked the Nauvoo City Charter to keep the Mormons in line. The Nauvoo Legion had been disbanded by state edict. "They were perceived as a threat, and sentiment . . . against them had become so vituperative that there was no way in the world they could be protected from their fellow Illinoisans," states Dr. Rodney Davis. "There wasn't any entity in the state that had the capacity to do that. The only peacekeeping enti-ty in the state of Illinois was the State Militia. And the State Militia could be politicized very easily. It was not a dispassionate non-partisan kind of peacekeeping entity, anything like what we perceive contemporary state police to be."

Brigham Young wrote an "epistle to the Church" declaring "the exodus of the nation of the only true Israel from these United States to a far distant region of the west." He described the

temple and it was the instructions of Joseph Smith, Jr., and of Brigham Young that it be com-pleted and then they could go to the next gath-ering of Zion."

Mormonism transformed itself from what might originally have been a sect with a single leader into a broad-based movement in perhaps a shorter period of time than almost any other known religious group. Dr. John Butler con-tends, "By the time of Smith's assassination it was already a broadly based religious movement, an institution of real power and authority within its own and among its own members, and that was extraordinary. That is one of the charac-teristics that sets Mormonism apart from almost all other new religious movements. Not only in the nineteenth century but in the history of religion generally. It was truly extraordinary."

8

CITY FOR

SALE

We completed the temple, used it a

short time, and were done with it.

On the 5th and 6th of February, 1846

we committed the building into

the hands of the Lord, and left it.[1]

— Brigham Young

Efforts not directed at completing the temple were focused on the trek west. Fifteen hundred wagons had been finished and another eighteen hundred were in process. Earlier that summer, Orson Hyde had traveled east to purchase canvas for a tabernacle structure near the temple. He had no funds but was able to raise $1,100 among the members of branches of the Church. When the four thousand yards of Russian duck canvas arrived, it was redirected for wagon covers and tents for the pilgrimage. So was the $125 worth of hemp bought specially to be used for the cords for the tabernacle.

The town throbbed with activity and anticipation. "Men were thick as blackbirds busily engaged upon the various portions [of the temple], all intent upon its completion although we were being in constant expectation of a mob," wrote Wandle Mace. "We labored while the wicked raged, the mobs howled, but they could not stop the work on the temple until it was so far completed that it was accepted of the Lord."[2]

"*It was both the project of building the temple and the experience spiritually within it that was the glue of the community and that also took them across the plains.*"

—DR. TRUMAN G. MADSEN

"Ye are no more strangers and foreigners, but fellow citizens with the saints, and of the household of God; And are built upon the foundation of the apostles and prophets, Jesus Christ himself being the chief corner stone; In whom all the building fitly framed together groweth unto an holy temple in the Lord." —Ephesians 2:19-21

BY LATE NOVEMBER 1845, the temple was nearly finished. The Saints in celebration enjoyed "a little season of recreation" in the temple. Musicians produced violins, flutes, and even a hornpipe and played several very good dancing tunes. The festivities in the temple were enjoyed but a short time. "I will not have division and contention, and I mean that there shall not be a fiddle in this Church but what has Holiness to the Lord upon it, nor a flute, nor a trumpet, nor any other instrument of music."[3] President Young insisted "they refrain from dancing in the sacred building lest the spirit of levity creep into their solemn meetings and mar the sanctity of the Lord's house."[4]

Sitting atop the temple's sculpted limestone was the frame attic, which was divided into two sections. A large boxlike structure with a relatively flat roof faced west; a rectangular hall stretched to the east, sheltered by small offices on each side. This floor was accessed by circular staircases in the northwest and southwest corners and lit by skylights in the gabled roof. A semi-circular window described as "truly magnificent" drew in light from the east in its twenty-foot span. It was here that the Saints would cluster to participate in sacred rites of worship.

With the financial pressures to prepare for an exodus west, furnishings and decorations for the temple were borrowed from the Saints' homes rather than purchased. Women endowed earlier by the Prophet Joseph readied the top floor of the temple for ceremonies, while Heber C. Kimball and his son hauled wagonloads of potted plants up the hillside and arranged them in attic rooms created with canvas partitions. Members stripped their homes of furniture, paintings, mirrors, maps, and rugs to decorate

Opposite: Zina Huntington Jacobs, who had watched her father labor on the temple 818 days wrote: "The gospel net has caught all and the building is fitly framed."[5] The sacrifices of the Nauvoo Saints bore sweet fruit.

the building and set the stage for the long-anticipated blessed ceremonies.

"One of the functions of a temple was certainly to help people who had built the temple and were in the community that used this building to . . . feel close to their God, and feel that their God could help them. And they did that in many ways. One of those ways was by providing for God the best that they had to offer in terms of the furnishings that they provided for the building," Dr. Carol Meyers notes.

On November 30, Brigham Young in the company of fellow Church leaders, dedicated the attic for sacred services, and called down help for those busily engaged getting ready for their departure, including wheelwrights, carpenters, cabinetmakers, wagon makers, mechanics, and blacksmiths. He recorded this prayer in his journal: "We trust in God, we praise him that we have been thus far able to prepare his Temple for the ordinances of the priesthood, and we feel full of confidence that he will hear our prayers and deliver his unoffending people from the power of their enemies where we can enjoy peace for a season."[6]

On December 10, the temple opened for sacred work. Early that morning, prior to the beginning of temple work, two Catholic officials toured the temple with, the Mormons hoped, the intent to purchase the structure. Later that afternoon, invitations were extended only to those who could produce receipts for their payment of tithes in full.

Thirty people attended the first session, which lasted until 3:30 the next morning. As group after group entered the temple, "it seemed the whole house was filled with angels."[7] That first group included well-known Church figures: Brigham Young and wife, Mary Ann; Heber C. Kimball and wife, Vilate; Orson Hyde and wife, Nancy Marinda; Parley P. Pratt and wife, Mary Ann; John Taylor and wife, Lenora; George A. Smith and wife Bathsheba. Hyrum Smith's widow Mary also joined the group as did the widow of Don Carlos Smith. For the next six weeks, Brigham Young and members of the Twelve and their wives administered the endowment to thousands of Saints.

THE CEREMONIES OF TEMPLE WORSHIP are strikingly similar to the kinds of activities that have taken place over time in the great temple-building cultures. They were an infusion of divine grace and a mode of covenant making, enabling the Saints to draw closer to the Lord Jesus Christ.

Day and night for six weeks, small companies of men and women entered "the house of the Lord" for what was to them long-awaited, hallowed worship. In his teachings, Joseph Smith had connected salvation—what so many had been seeking—with the rituals of the temple.

"As the people of Nauvoo prepared themselves to go to the temple and receive their endowments," Dr. Glen Leonard explains, "they examined their lives to make sure they were pure and worthy and holy to enter that special house. So that they would go in there with an open heart to be taught and to make covenants and promises to the Lord, expecting His blessings."

"It was the most interesting scene of all my life and one that afforded the most peace and joy since we were married," said Norton Jacobs who had worked at many tasks to construct the temple.[8] He and his wife were endowed in one of the first companies. In the weeks ahead, "most of the saints, men and women, had the privilege of receiving their endowments, learning the order of the priesthood and the fall and redemption of man in the Temple in the City of Joseph. Nauvoo was called by that name after the death of Joseph," wrote John Pulsipher. "It was accepted of the Lord, and His holy angels have ministered unto many therein."[9] On the last day of temple work, James H. Rollins and his wife "went through with a great throng of people." Rollins had assisted Joseph Smith in preparing the Red Brick Store for the first instructions in the endowment in May 1842.[10]

"This temple marks the very epitome of our worship which we believe came through revelation to the Prophet Joseph Smith. And which means so very much," President Gordon B. Hinckley states. "All that takes place within this temple is concerned with the things of the spirit of man, an eternal being; the continuity of the family, and the relationships that can exist on the other side, just as they exist here."

IMP

MANY NEWSPAPERS CARRIED ACCOUNTS and impressions of the curious who had visited the Nauvoo Temple. Adding to the draw was its remote location and its cost of close to $1 million. The *New York Sun* reported, "The building of the Mormon Temple under all the troubles by which those people have been surrounded, seems to be carried on with a religious enthusiasm which reminds us of olden times."[11] The *Advocate* of Columbus, Ohio, claimed the Mormon temple "now building, will probably in beauty of design, extent and durability, excel any public building in the state."[12] The *Salem Advertiser* applauded the temple as "different from anything in ancient or modern history."[13]

John Greenleaf Whittier gave the temple a status even more grand, suggesting it would be "the most splendid and imposing architectural monument in the New World."[14]

Joseph Smith's hometown newspaper in Palmyra, New York, ever on the alert for news of the Mormons since their founding of the Church in that vicinity years before, published a detailed description of the temple's appearance in 1847:

> A stately Temple erected at a cost of $750,000, has grown up and run to decay within the brief period of ten years!—a fresh warning against building on "sandy foundations." . . . The first sight we had of it gave us a pang of disappointment, for it looked more like a white Yankee meeting house, with its steeple on one end, than a magnificent structure that had cost, all uncompleted as it is, seven hundred and fifty thousand dollars. But as we approached nearer, it proved to be something worth seeing. It is nearly a mile from the landing, the most conspicuous, in fact the only conspicuous object in the city.
>
> It is built of white lime-stone. The front is ornamented with sunken square columns of no particular style of architecture, having capitals representing half a man's head—the upper half—showing the forehead, and the top of the nose, and crowned with thorns, or perhaps what was intended for the points of stars.
>
> Over the head are two bugles or horns, with their largest ends outwards, and the handles, or the upper side, forming a sort of festoon protection. On all sides of the Temple are similar columns and similar capitals. The base of each column is heavy, but in good proportion and of a fanciful design, which it would be difficult to describe.
>
> There is a basement with small windows. Ten steps lead to the font and only one entrance to the main building. Three arches enable you to enter into a sort of vestibule, from which, by doors, you enter the grand hall, and at the side are the entries to the staircases, to ascend to the upper apartments.

The front of the Temple is apparently three stories high, and is surmounted by an octagonal tower or steeple, which itself is three stories, with a dome and having on four sides a clock next below the dome. There is a line of circular windows over the arched entrance, ornamented with carved work between each, and over that again a line of square entablature, on which is cut the following inscription:

THE HOUSE OF THE LORD BUILT BY THE CHURCH OF JESUS CHRIST OF LATTER-DAY SAINTS
Commenced April 6th, 1841
Holiness to the Lord

A similar entablature is on the front of the interior vestibule, over the doors of the entrance with the same inscription. The letters are gilt.

We were then taken to the very top of the building, and enjoyed there, for sometime, a view of the surrounding country, which, of itself, well paid for the trouble of ascending, as the whole valley of the Mississippi for miles and miles lay exposed to view.

Coming down, we were ushered into the Council Chamber, which is a large, low room, lighted by one large half circle window at the end and several small sky-lights in the roof. On each side are six antechambers, said to have been intended for twelve priests, councillors, or elders.

In the entry on each side of the door to the Council Chamber, is a room called the wardrobe, where the priests were to keep their dresses. On one side was a room intended for a pantry, showing that the priests did not mean to go supperless to bed. Under the Council Chamber another large hall, with seven windows on each side, and four at the farther end.

On the lower floor was a grand hall for the assemblage and worship of the people. Over the window at the end, was inscribed, in gilded capital letters:

THE LORD HAS BEHELD OUR SACRIFICE
COME AFTER US

This was in a circular line corresponding to the circle of the ceiling. Seats are provided in this hall for the accommodation of thirty-five hundred people, and they are arranged with backs, which are fitted like the seats in a modern railroad car, so as to allow the spectator to sit and look in either direction, east or west.

At the east and west ends are raised platforms, composed of series of pulpits, on steps one above the other. The fronts of these pulpits are semi-circular, and are inscribed in gilded letters on the west side, PAP, PPQ, PTQ, meaning as we are informed, the uppermost one President of Aaronic Priesthood; the second, President of the Priests Quorum; the third, President of the Teachers Quorum; and the fourth and lowest, President of the Deacons Quorum. On the east side the pulpits are marked PHP, PHQ, PSR, and the knowledge of the guide was no better than ours as to what these symbolic letters were intended for.

We next descended to the basement, where is the far-celebrated font. It is in fact the cellar of the building. The font is of white limestone, of an oval shape, twelve by sixteen feet in size on the inside, and about four and a half to five feet deep. It is very plain and rests on the back of twelve stone oxen or cows, which stand immersed to their knees in the earth.

It has two flights of steps, with iron bannisters, by which you enter and go out of the font, one at the east end, and the other at the west end. The oxen have tin horns and tin ears, but are otherwise of stone, and a stone drapery hangs like a curtain down from the font, so as to prevent the exposure of all back of the forelegs of the beasts. In consequence of what I had heard of this font I was disappointed; for it was neither vast nor gorgeous; everything about it was quite simple and unostentatious. The basement is unpaved, and on each side and at the ends are small alcoves, intended for robing rooms for the faithful.

The whole is quite unfinished, and one can imagine what it might have been in course of time, if Joe Smith had been allowed to pursue his career in prosperity.[15]

"Given the fact that the temple is a duplication or representation or re-creation on earth of a heavenly temple, a part of heaven itself, it implies the most holy and sacred environment," Dr. John Lundquist suggests. "The requirements are that those who wish to enter the temple sanctify themselves, they consecrate themselves, they'd be living a holy life. And almost always it implies and requires special clothing and preparations of that nature to enter into that sacred space."

The sentiments of Erastus Snow express the sentiments of so many: "The Spirit, Power, and Wisdom of God reigned continually in the Temple and all felt satisfied that during the two months we occupied it in the endowments of the Saints, we were amply paid for all our labors in building it."[16]

The Saints were so anxious to receive the promised blessings that Brigham reported, "I have given myself up entirely to the work of the Lord in the Temple night and day, not taking more than four hours sleep, upon an average, per day, and going home but once a week."[17] Shifts in the temple lasted around the clock as did preparation for the exodus. Men and women worked long hours—some both day and night—those winter weeks to administer ordinances before the exodus. Those attending the temple brought lunches and dinners for themselves as well as for those who were serving full-time. They lingered, wanting to draw upon the spirit they felt within the walls they had sacrificed so much to construct. "I worked in the Temple every day without cessation until it was closed," recalled Elizabeth Ann Whitney, one of thirty-six women workers. "I gave myself, my time and attention to that mission."[18]

Special clothing for the temple needed to be made. Dr. Jacob Neusner states, "Scripture is explicit that Israel is a kingdom of Priests and a holy people. Therefore we aren't surprised that scripture designates a particular kind of clothing or something to affix to clothing, which marks the people as holy." Several dozen women attended to the sewing and washing of clothing; at one point some items hanging too close to the wood burning stoves caught fire causing more alarm than damage.

While the Mormons were enjoying a season of spiritual rejuvenation, their enemies continued to press them but with little success. Guards patrolled the temple at night and residents were prepared to rally at the "tolling of the Temple bell." At the alarm, the men were to meet at the parade ground armed and equipped to protect Nauvoo. The Quincy Riflemen marched into what they called "the holy city" unannounced one day hoping to make some arrests. They wait-

"You knew that something important, something of cosmic significance took place in the temple and that gave it stature."

—DR. EDWIN S. GAUSTAD

ed two hours on the square before marching to the temple and dispatching a few of the brigade to search it. Their efforts were futile and they then marched two miles out of the city and camped. The officer in charge reported the night "was fine, but cold and windy."[19]

Zina Diantha Huntington recorded her thoughts as the strain mounted: "When I cast mine eyes out, what do I behold? Every brother armed, his gun upon his shoulder to protect his family and brethren from the violence of the furious mob who are now burning all that falls into their way round about the Country. Ah Liberty, thou art fled. When the wicked rule, the people mourn."[20]

Below: Actual minutes recording the march of the Quincy Riflemen into Nauvoo. They hoped to arrest President Brigham Young, but a clever ruse devised by President Young and William Miller foiled their efforts.

What had the marauders hoped to find? "I think people were jealous and resentful of their economic prosperity, of their cohesiveness as a social group and a political group," Dr. Truman Madsen states. "They also distrusted the religion because, here again, you have the example of the temple. And, outsiders don't know what's going on in the temple. And what you don't know about you fear and you imagine all sorts of things."

Arrest warrants circulated for members of the Twelve on trumped-up charges of counterfeiting. One brisk evening, a U.S. Marshall flanked by a dozen soldiers appeared at the temple, hoping to grab Brigham Young when he left. Brigham asked William Miller "an excellent man and perfectly reliable," to distract them. Miller donned Brigham's cape, went out to Brigham's carriage and was immediately detained. Exultant, the posse took him to Carthage, announcing, "We've got him." While in custody at an Inn, Miller was recognized. Said a local farmer, "That's not Brigham; that is William Miller, one of my old neighbors."[21] Miller was released. Of the persecutors one of the faithful said, "May God grant that they may always be foiled in their attempts and fall into their own pit which they have prepared for the Saints."[22]

Although the Temple was now in full use, it was still unfinished. At one Sunday meeting, the message of the speaker was interrupted. "A slight crack was heard in the floor and being laid on truss girders they settled a little. . . . Suddenly the people began to scream as though they expected the house to fall in on them instantly. They rushed in every direction and some began to break the sash and glass. Thus several windows were broken and men plunged out like mad cats upon the frozen ground and stones below. 'Twas in vain to attempt to restore order and President Young directed the people to go out into the grove."[23]

The ordinance work of the temple including marriage ceremonies called sealings continued into February 1846. Helen Mar Whitney spoke of her eventful day saying, "At early twilight on the 3rd of February a messenger was sent by my father, informing H. K. Whitney and myself that . . . we were to present ourselves there that evening. The weather being fine we preferred to walk; and as we passed through the little graveyard at the foot of the hill a solemn covenant we entered into—to cling to each other through time and, if permitted, throughout all eternity."[24]

Threatened with military intervention, Brigham Young and Church authorities chose to abandon Nauvoo earlier than expected. The first wagons of an advance party began rolling down Parley's Street to the river on February 4, 1846. About a week later, the temperature dropped, freezing the waters of the Mississippi and allowing numerous caravans of exiles to cross the ice

Opposite: The Latter-day Saints would sacrifice on the trail west in search of a place which God had prepared for His people. It was popular for artists of this time to idealize scenery—thus explaining the mountains in the background, although none actually exist.

Below: Tools the Saints took with them to the West.

into Iowa. The evacuation was arduous and painful and lasted until fall. "We commenced crossing the river, the weather being very cold and with large quantities of ice running in the

would leave it in His hands to do as He pleased; and to preserve the building as a monument to Joseph Smith. We asked the Lord to accept the labors of His servants in this land."[26]

Brigham had intended to lead the train into Iowa. But at the temple, a throng of Saints were waiting, hoping to receive entry. At this point, Brigham promised temple blessings when they reached their new home but as he strode away, he turned. "Looking upon the multitude and knowing their anxiety, as they were thirsting and hungering for the word, we continued at work diligently in the House of the Lord."[27] He

"IT IS IRONIC THAT THE SAINTS SPENT FIVE YEARS BUILDING THE TEMPLE AND THEN JUST SIX WEEKS RECEIVING THEIR ENDOWMENTS AND BLESSING AND THEN WALKED AWAY FROM IT. BUT THEY DID IT WILLINGLY BECAUSE THEY HAD RECEIVED THOSE BLESSINGS, AND BRIGHAM YOUNG PROMISED THEM THAT THEY WOULD BUILD EVEN A GRANDER TEMPLE OUT THERE IN THE WILDERNESS WHEN THEY GOT THERE TO THE NEW GATHERING PLACE."

—DR. GLEN M. LEONARD

river," said John Smith of the initial exodus. "We leave in the City of Nauvoo a good house of brick and a quantity of good furniture, without making a sale of anything."[25]

Before leaving in the advance party, Brigham Young and members of the Quorum of the Twelve quietly presented the temple to the Lord. He later recorded that they knelt, "and dedicated the building to the Most High. We asked His blessing upon our intended move to the west; also we asked Him to enable us some day to finish the Temple, and dedicate it to Him, and we

returned to the temple and another 600 received their rites in those last hours.

Lining up for temple blessings added to the disconnection between the Mormon and the non-Mormon citizenry. "You heard about the ritual whether or not you knew what it was," states Dr. Edwin S. Gaustad.

The temple served the people well, though by most standards they had hardly used it. "I might ask why it is that we have been to all this outlay and expense, such as building the temple, and then are called to leave it," Ara Sabin said of the five-year project. "I would answer that the people of God always were required to make sacrifices . . . worthy of the people of God. We do not want to leave a desolate place to be a reproach to us, but something that will be a monument of our industry and virtue."[28]

Records show that nearly 6,000 people received their endowments in the Nauvoo Temple. "They were both prepared for death, which they were taught could be sweet unto them," explains Dr. Madsen, "and they were prepared for life and the arduous pattern that they had to undertake."

In harsh winter weather, reminiscent of their flight from Missouri, the Latter-day Saints

thousand homes, businesses, and fields of grain. "The Temple of the Lord is left solitary in the midst of our enemies," said Brigham Young.[31] With a sure understanding of the danger the Saints were leaving behind and the uncertainty of the journey before them, President Young concluded, "To save the lives of all the Saints from cruel murder, we moved westward."[32]

President Gordon B. Hinckley said of their exit, "They were driven out, they had no alternative. The government did not defend them. They were at the mercy of the mobs, their enemies. They had no place to go."

"The top of this hill, I was aware, was the last point from which I could see the Nauvoo

"I absolutely marvel at Brigham Young, at his courage, his vision to lead thousands upon thousands of people into an uncharted wilderness. It is a miracle to me."

—President Gordon B. Hinckley

evacuated what had been their home. Eliza R. Snow penned her thoughts saying, "The wrath and bloodthirsty spirit of our enemies, sustained and encouraged by State authority, at this time predominated to that degree that the labors in the Temple were closed, and the energies of the Saints directed towards a hasty flight. . . . to what point we did not know, but go we must."[29]

Their enemies watched with curiosity and little compassion; the mass exodus would become the largest westward migration in American history. Said Illinois resident James L. Blanchard, "So much confusion for the last two or three weeks. The way the Mormons have shelled out of Nauvoo is a sight. I hope not to see many such scenes."[30]

Left behind was the stately temple, several

Temple." wrote Priddy Meeks as he began the grueling journey. "I have no words with which to convey a proper conception of my feelings when taking a last look at this sacred monument of the living faith of the Saints, and which was associated in their minds with the heavenly and the holy."[33]

The pages of the *Quincy Whig* said of the exit: "The Mormons are leaving with all possible haste. During the week 400 teams and 1350 souls have gone; others are preparing to leave as fast as possible."[34] Thomas Sharp reveled in the departure, editorializing in the *Warsaw Signal*, "Now that the Mormons are gone, we can get back to peace and quiet again."[35] Said Brigham Young of the time, "We completed a temple in Kirtland and in Nauvoo and did not the bells of hell toll all the time. . . . They did, every week and every day."[36]

Not everyone in that early spring of 1846 headed west into Iowa, though the hope expressed in the *Hancock Eagle* was that "in due season" all "depart upon their pilgrimage towards the setting sun."[37] Some of the most trusted Church leaders remained behind until May to try to finish the temple and publicly dedicate it to God. Mormon Samuel Richards who joined the throng of nearly 9,000 attending the dedication wrote, "Friday May 1. The Nauvoo temple was dedicated in the presence of strangers and all who would pay $1 admittance. I was one of three who was appointed to seat the congregation in the House, and stood part of the time at the door to receive tickets."[38]

Wilford Woodruff who had the assignment to oversee the solemn dedication wrote, "I was taking a final farewell of Nauvoo for this life. I looked upon the Temple and City of Nauvoo as they receded from view and asked the Lord to remember the sacrifices of his saints."[39]

The *Hancock Eagle* announced the late spring departure: "The Twelve with their thousands of followers have abandoned their Temple and their city; with them, goes all that the enemies of Mormonism regard as inimical to the genius of our institutions and the well being of the community at large."[40]

But a pocket of the faithful stayed behind. Too poor, too sick to face the trek, they had been trying to muster teams and supplies for the journey. In June 1846, hostile parties from Warsaw, Quincy, and Carthage renewed efforts to banish the few remaining Mormons. Thomas Gregg, a leading anti-Mormon in Warsaw, noted, "It began to be feared that many of the Mormons were not intending to leave the city, but to quietly remain, in the hope and expectation that in time the danger would be over."[41]

September 10, Nauvoo was under siege. Colonel Thomas Brockman and his troops bombarded the city with cannon fire; they stormed homes, roadways, and farms. A later report described the events: "Finding that our number in Nauvoo were reduced to a mere handful, the mob, numbering some 1800 armed men . . .

attacked the remaining few who were chiefly lame, blind, widows, fatherless children and those too poor to get away."[42] Ann Eliza Coffin, seven years old at the time spoke of seeing "the army coming into the town of Nauvoo . . . the cannon ball roll past our door."[43] The assailants cannonaded the citizenry of Nauvoo for three days; the beleaguered residents returned fire but they were no match for the aggressors.

The *Burlington Iowa Hawkeye* reported, "Whatever can be done should be done speedily in bringing this civil war and bloodshed to an end . . . last Friday a cannonading took place between the anti-Mormons and the Mormons and new settler forces. Saturday a general battle took place. Last night (Sunday) the roar of artillery which followed each other in rapid succession and which we hear distinctly in the town evinced that the third deadly strife was going on."[44]

"THE TEMPLE WAS SACRED TO THE LATTER-DAY SAINTS AND THEY KEPT PEOPLE OUT WHO WERE NOT RIGHTEOUS, HONORABLE, PEACE SEEKING PEOPLE. SO, WHEN THE VIGILANTES CAME IN AND CHASED THE LAST OF THE SAINTS OUT, AND OCCUPIED IT AND VULGARIZED IT, VANDALIZED IT, THIS ARMY OF OCCUPATION IN A SENSE WAS MAKING IT A HEADQUARTERS AND IT WAS A WAY OF DESACRALIZING THE TEMPLE."

—Dr. Glen M. Leonard

The troops not only wanted dominion over the town, they wanted the temple, "a source of envy to the enemies of the Saints."[45] They took possession of the temple, marching around exultant in their conquest. The Saints watched with horror "seeing the mob take possession of the Temple and how they climbed on the outside of the railing . . . and marched around."[46]

Henry I. Young gave the temple keys to the chairman of the Quincy Committee, and the last

KEYS TO THE N

of the Mormon faithful fled Nauvoo in a sorry caravan. "Sick men and women were carried upon their beds, weary mothers with helpless babes dying in their arms hurried away," said Mason Brayman of the scene, "They scarcely knew or cared whither, so it was from their enemies, whom they feared more than the waves of the Mississippi, or the heat and hunger and lingering life and dreaded death of the prairies on which they were about to be cast. The ferry boats were crowded, and the river bank was lined with anxious fugitives, sadly awaiting their turn to pass over and take up their solitary march to the wilderness."[47]

Yet they felt prepared. "If it had not been for the faith and knowledge that was bestowed upon us in that temple by the influence and help of the spirit of the Lord, our journey would have been like one taking a leap in the dark," said Sarah Rich, "and in our state of poverty, it would seem like walking into the jaws of death."[48]

Said Brigham Young, "We will go to a land where there are at least no old settlers to quarrel with us; where we can say we have killed the snakes and made the roads, and we will leave this wicked nation to themselves for they have rejected the gospel. . . . This church has obtained already all they have labored for in building this temple, but after we leave here (I feel it in my bones) there will be thousands of men that can go into any part of the world and build up the kingdom, and build temples."[49]

Scholars have studied the connection between the building of the temple and then deserting it, venturing into the unknown frontier. "It's one of the great moments in our history that a people who already knew that they would be going into the wilderness, stayed behind to complete the temple, to dedicate it, and then to enter it, seeking for divine bless-

Right: This set of sixteen keys were reportedly used to open interior doors in the Nauvoo Temple. Brigham Young recommended that the Mormon caretakers—when making their exit from Nauvoo—leave the keys in the hands of a local judge, and the temple in the hands of the Lord. For years this set of keys has been on display in the Wood Museum in Quincy, Illinois.

Keys to The Old Mormon Temple

Upon departure of the Mormons from Nauvoo, these keys were given to Mr. Artois Hamilton by the Elders of the church, for safe keeping and in appreciation for the tender care Mr. Hamilton gave the bodies of Joseph and Hyrum Smith after they were killed in Carthage, Illinois, on June 27th 1844.

Presented by S. Bentley Hamilton.

ings," explains Dr. Truman Madsen. "I am certain the Prophet Joseph believed, that if they were going to make it across the desert and up into the mountains they needed to be endowed. . . . The temple was their redemptive power to make that wilderness journey. . . . They had come in touch with the Lord, and that was enough to keep them going."

Dr. John Butler adds that the Mormons were sustained by their "belief in Joseph Smith's vision, the sustaining belief in the vision of Mormonism as true Christianity as leading to as perfect and wonderful a society as any Christian could want," and they risked their lives to "head for a west of which they knew almost nothing."

Looking back at their circumstances, President Hinckley states, "The temple represented the acme of their gospel teachings and principles. It was concerned with the things of immortality, the things of eternity, the continuity of the human family, things that meant so very much to these people. It was there in that sacred house that under the authority of the holy priesthood those ordinances were administered which gave to them the strength and conviction to move forward in the great undertaking which was ahead of them. So very many of them gave their lives as a testimony of the conviction which they carried in their hearts."

Hundreds of miles west in Iowa, the Nauvoo residents were "without a home, dwelling in tents and wagons exposed to the inclemency of the weather." Wrote Isaac Haight, "We are even like the saints of old having no abiding city but we are wanderers and pilgrims on the earth."[50] Wandle Mace was one of the last to leave Nauvoo. A convert from the east, he had joined the Saints in Quincy and devoted his Nauvoo years to the building of the temple. His words and feelings were no doubt shared by thousands:

> Farewell Nauvoo the Beautiful, The
> City of Joseph! The home of so much
> joy and happy contentment, and also of
> the exquisite sorrow and anguish; here I
> enjoyed the association of our beloved
> Prophet, and Patriarch. . . . Farewell to
> the temple upon which I have labored

with so much pleasure, the second temple erected to the only true and living God. . . . This was built by the energy, tithes and offerings of an honest, although a poor, persecuted people.[51]

The Mormons had hoped to sell the temple to finance their journey. Though there was interest, there were no buyers. One newspaper peddled the idea of a purchase: "If any wealthy individual can be found who has a thirst for immortality he can slake it by purchasing this great edifice for some literary, religious or charitable institution."[52] A newspaper in Keokuk just across the river from Nauvoo stated, "Strangers from all parts of the country were

The words were prophetic, for the temple did not stand long.

The work of an arsonist, October 9, 1848 brought down the grand structure. On "a beautiful night, [at] about three o'clock in the morning fire was discovered in the cupola. It . . . spread rapidly, and in a very short period the lofty spire was a mass of flame, shooting high in the air, and illuminating a wide extent of country. . . . citizens gathered around, but nothing could be done to save the structure. . . . In two hours, and before the sun dawned upon the earth, the proud structure, reared at so much cost—and a monument of religious zeal— stood with blackened and smoldering walls."[56] The interior has been "like a furnace; the walls of

"I WOULD RATHER IT SHOULD THUS BE DESTROYED THAN REMAIN IN THE HANDS OF THE WICKED." —Brigham Young

attracted to the place, to see this monument of misdirected labor and religious error." The *New York Sun* said of the deserted building, "History may be unable to explain what race worshiped there."[53] The place was taken over by Etienne Cabet and his Icarians who intended to use it as a seminary for their people. Their plans were never realized.

Brigham Young's good-bye was heartfelt: "The temple of the Lord is left solitary in the midst of our enemies, an enduring monument of the diligence and integrity of the Saints."[54]

Nauvoo, once a boomtown, now was still. The temple, which a St. Louis newspaper had described as "the most extraordinary building on the American continent," stood vacant—its glory short-lived.

For some, the temple still had purpose as suggested by a Burlington newspaper comment: "As long as it stands, the Temple will continue to be a great attraction of the upper Mississippi."[55]

solid masonry heated throughout and cracked by the intense heat." For days, the solid masonry walls were "too hot to be touched."[57]

A message to Salt Lake carried the news of the fire. Brigham Young responded, "I would rather it should thus be destroyed than remain in the hands of the wicked. If it be the will of the Lord that the temple be burned . . . God commanded us to build the Nauvoo Temple, and we built it, and performed our duty pretty well.[58]

Two years later, a tornado toppled all but one wall of the remaining structure. Curiosity seekers, enterprising contractors, and scavengers sold or carted off the manicured stone for use in walls and foundations in all parts of the country. Said the *Carthage Republican*, "The last remaining vestige of what the famous Mormon temple was in its former glory has disappeared, and nothing now remains to mark its site but heaps of broken stone and rubbish."[59]

The pride of Nauvoo was gone. For a time.

"I think [the temple] built within them a certain knowledge concerning the truth of the cause in which they were engaged and that adherence to the principles to which they had subscribed was more important than life itself. In accordance with that conviction which they carried in their hearts, which had been solidified in the experiences they had in that temple, they left their homes, they picked up their goods, they drove their wagons down to the river, crossed the river and headed west never to return to Nauvoo or to set their sights on the city of their dreams again."

—President Gordon B. Hinckley

9

COME
AFTER US

"The new building will stand as a memorial to those who built the first such structure there on the banks of the Mississippi."

—Gordon B. Hinckley

IN THE AUTUMN OF 1846, Colonel Thomas L. Kane landed alone at the wharf of Nauvoo. He recounted the eerie atmosphere:

"No one met me there. I looked, and saw no one. I could hear no one move, though the quiet everywhere was such that I heard the flies buzz, and the water-ripples break against the shallow of the beach. I walked through the solitary street. . . . The Mormons in Nauvoo and its dependencies had been numbered the year before at over twenty thousand. Where were they? They had last been seen carrying in mournful train their sick and wounded, halt and blind, to disappear behind the western horizon, pursuing the phantom of another home. Hardly anything else was known of them: and people asked with curiosity, 'What had been their fate—what their fortunes?'"[1]

Exiled, they had only one place to go—across the river into the territory of Iowa—and west. It was a wild, untamed land with few roads or settlements. The Mormons asked James Clarke, Iowa Territorial Governor, to grant them safe passage. Unlike Governor Boggs of Missouri and Governor Ford of Illinois, whose anti-Mormon positions caused the near collapse of the Church, Governor Clarke promised them safety and fulfilled his pledge.

These latter-day children of Israel spent the next winter in makeshift quarters on the western edge of the state in a settlement they named Winter Quarters. In the spring of 1847, a vanguard company led by Brigham Young pushed across the Great Plains to the desert valleys of the Great Basin. For the next three decades, streams of new converts followed their trail to a new Zion, "far away in the West." They built towns and enterprises, homes, farms, schools—and temples.

It couldn't have been easy. They went from the buzz of building the Nauvoo Temple to a wandering life on the wilderness trail. Before the winter evacuation, they inscribed in gold capital letters on the wall of the grand Assembly Hall, "THE LORD HAS BEHELD OUR SACRIFICE, COME AFTER US." Those words said so much about their time in Nauvoo. Dr. Truman Madsen explains that the phrase had a double meaning: "It meant even after all we have sacrificed to build this, we must leave it. Not

COME, COME, YE SAINTS,
NO TOIL NOR LABOR FEAR;
BUT WITH JOY WEND YOUR WAY.
THOUGH HARD TO YOU THIS JOURNEY MAY APPEAR,
GRACE SHALL BE AS YOUR DAY.
'TIS BETTER FAR FOR US TO STRIVE
OUR USELESS CARES FROM US TO DRIVE;
DO THIS, AND JOY YOUR HEARTS WILL SWELL —
ALL IS WELL! ALL IS WELL!

—William Clayton

only that, once you have come and made the covenants we have made, then the explanation and the outcome of your covenant will be to join us in the conquest of the Great Basin."

Brigham Young promised the Saints as they were packing to abandon Nauvoo and their temple, "We shall come back here and we shall . . . build [temples] all over the continent of North America."[2]

Opposite: The first builders of the Nauvoo Temple left a legacy of grit, ingenuity, resilience, and unbounded devotion to the Almighty.

Come After Us

The Mormons dedicated ground for a temple in Salt Lake just days after the first caravan arrived in the valley. It took 40 years to build; many of the Nauvoo laborers applied their experience to the Salt Lake edifice. Since its dedication in 1893, it has become a visible symbol of Mormon commitment to the divine. Three other temples were completed in the meantime and more temples followed not only on the American continent but all around the world. "We've now built and operate 106 temples across the world," President Hinckley said of the forward march through two centuries of temple construction. "We've reached a point," he explains, "where we can go back and re-create the past without losing sight of the challenges and the opportunities of the future."

> *"The Mormons haven't always been treated well in Nauvoo. There is still some resistance but we're warming up to their presence. . . . I treasure my relationship with the Mormons."*
>
> —LeRoy A. Ufkes, Carthage, Illinois, Attorney

Fifty-two years after the Saints had surrendered Nauvoo, Arza Erastus Hinckley, a young laborer on the Temple and a great-uncle of President Gordon B. Hinckley, said, "We have not got back to the starting place yet, but that must soon be."[3] It took another one hundred years.

THE IDEA OF REBUILDING the historic Nauvoo Temple had surfaced before. President Hinckley's father, Bryant, who was the LDS mission president over the Nauvoo area in 1939, proposed rebuilding the historic temple. Having just come out of the Depression, the Church did not act upon his suggestion. It is curious that President Hinckley in his great push to complete temples around the world would preside over the rebuilding of this remarkable structure. "I count it something of a strange and wonderful coincidence," he states, "that I've had a part in the determination of rebuilding this temple."

But it is Joseph Smith who is most pleased with the rebuilding of the temple, according to President Hinckley: "This was his crowning objective. This was the great desire of his heart. This represented his final great effort."

The Nauvoo Temple "occupies a unique place in history and in the interest of our people," President Hinckley states. "It represents a backward look, a peek into our history, restoring the memories of the past." He further suggested, "The Nauvoo Temple might represent to the world a recognition of the maturity of this Church in its history. It says that we are aware and conscious and grateful for a great history that lies behind us. And that we are aware and conscious of a great opportunity and challenge which lies ahead of us. And this restoration stands as something of a monument to that maturity in the Church."

"The rebuilding of any sanctuary on the ruins of one that preceded it is really quite remarkable but also quite typical of temples in the ancient world," Dr. Carol Meyers points out. "This contemporary practice resonates with what people did thousands of years ago. There were buildings that were rebuilt after having been destroyed time and time again." Such a place is, she suggests, "where God's presence would easily come to rest."

"Nauvoo, for more than a hundred years, had been a 'quiet' hamlet. The LDS announcement changed that; the community of 1,200 residents braced for religious pilgrims. The Mormons haven't always been treated well in Nauvoo,"

Opposite: From a front window of today's Nauvoo Temple, the setting sun acts as a reminder of the close of an era—days marked by the mournful march of a persecuted people.

states LeRoy A. Ufkes, a resident of nearby Carthage. "There is always some resistance, but we're warming up to their presence. They are not a pushy group and have bent over backwards to be helpful. In fact, all of us are invited to view the temple interior before the public open house begins."

The LDS groundbreaking ceremony of 24 October 1999 drew more than 4,600 people and put in motion a massive rebuilding project with a fast-track schedule. As with its predecessor, the Nauvoo Temple was built by the donations of Church members. Cash came in large and small sums including penny drives by children. Doctors, lawyers, college professors, farmers, bankers, and businessmen all volunteered their time. But it was a steady crew, a couple of hundred at its peak, who reconstructed the hallowed

edifice. Their efforts mirrored the expressions of their counterparts two centuries ago: "There is no sacrifice required at the hand of the people of God but it shall be rewarded to them an hundred fold in time or in eternity."[4]

From the outset of the rebuilding of the Nauvoo Temple, the Church has paid attention to meaningful dates and events related to the initial construction of the building and culminating in the dedication. The three-day services are slated to begin on the anniversary of the Prophet Joseph's martyrdom, June 27, 1844. While the temple dedication in May 1846 was open to the public for a small fee, this dedication will be broadcast by satellite to congregations of faithful Saints around the world. The highlight of the services will be a prayer of dedication of this most significant "House of the Lord." The Mormon Tabernacle

"THERE'S A CERTAIN SANCTITY ATTACH
THAT'S WHERE THE TEMPLE STOOD; THA
RESTED. I BELIEVE THAT GROUND IS SAC

RESTORING THE MEI

More than 4,600 people attended the Groundbreaking Ceremony on Oct. 24, 1999 with construction beginning in February 2000. More than one thousand employees and volunteers worked on the temple site in the more than two years of construction.

By March 9, 2000 the foundation's 67 caissons were in place—12 to 25 feet deep—and workmen began pouring the floors. The original walls were stone-on-stone masonry construction; the new temple is made of reinforced concrete with the limestone veneer bolted to a thick stainless steel framework.

Great ingenuity was required to fit all the mechanical equipment for a modern LDS temple into a nineteenth century building. By September 2000 the walls had reached the fourth floor.

By November 2000, the exterior walls had reached the roof line. The elliptical window on the east side—19 feet long and 7 feet tall—was not installed in January 2002. According to Window Designer Charles Allen the massive insulated window includes the smallest pane of exterior glass: one and half inches long by one and a quarter inches wide.

Choir will sing a Mormon hymn composed by early Church member William W. Phelps, which has been sung at temple dedications since the first in Kirtland, Ohio.

A cornerstone ceremony on 5 November 2000 hearkened back "as nearly as possible" to the pageantry of the April 6, 1841 event. The four cornerstones weighed 1,400 pounds each. President Hinckley commented at their placement, "My wife was asleep when I left this morning and I left a note for her. It said, 'Have gone to Nauvoo. Will be back at 4:30 this afternoon.' Now, that's a miracle. If I had said to Brigham Young, 'Brigham, I'm going home this afternoon. It will take me two hours and ten minutes.' He would say, 'You're out of your head' because he never could have imagined, never could have dreamed that we would fly through

the sky at . . . 550 miles an hour in coming to this place which they left with such sorrow, such misery and such regret long ago."

In a prayer, President Hinckley petitioned the Lord that the temple "may become a holy site for Thy people across the world, that they may wish to come here and to enter this holy house and here engage in the ordinances of the gospel and also reflect on what occurred here in this city of Nauvoo."[5] He was followed by President Boyd K. Packer who drew the distinction, "The temple died. But now, this day it has come to a resurrection. The temple stands here again."[6]

By January 2000, more than one hundred and fifty years following the mass exodus, the temple began to rise again on the bluff above the Mississippi. While the original was constructed entirely of limestone, the walls of the new tem-

O TO A DEDICATED PIECE OF GROUND. . . .

S WHERE ALL THE HOPES OF THE SAINTS

ED GROUND."
                        —PRESIDENT GORDON B. HINCKLEY

IORIES OF THE PAST

By January 2001 the exterior of the temple was ready to receive the finish stone and windows. The first block of limestone veneer was secured on the south wall May 2, 2001. The first window was installed in the basement level on the south side May 8, 2001.

Individual pieces of limestone veneer were connected to a stainless steel frame and bolted to the concrete building. Each stone was numbered for placement. The outside of the temple includes 12,205 polished limestones.

On July 3, 2001 the bell was hoisted up to the temple tower. It was hung and rung on August 21, 2001.
Right: On December 3, 2001 the last of the 90 ornamental stones, a starstone, was secured to the temple and the last star window was hung. There are 330 stars on the temple including the starstones, star windows and ornamental stars on the balusters and tower.

Top Right: The star is a consistent artistic feature on the temple in both art glass and the stained glass on the exterior. The exterior red, white, and blue star windows of the original temple and the rebuilt structure are held in place with wood mullions rather than the stained-glass technique.

Right: Each piece of glass in a decorative panel is numbered to assure that the precise pattern is shaped. The glass is then soldered into place using a mixture of lead and tin. Holdman and four assistants worked full-time for more than a year to complete the two windows. They were joined by two hundred volunteers who had the painstaking task of edging the hundreds of pieces of handblown glass with copper-foil tape.

The celestial room skylight, which took four months to complete, has eight panels, and each one includes eighty-two pieces of glass. The entire window is composed of 656 pieces of colored, antique glass. The original temple included such a skylight, though it was not completed in decorative glass.

Above: Each window is first sketched in meticulous detail as a pattern for the antique glass creation. The window for the baptistry is a scene picturing the baptism of Jesus Christ in the Jordan River. This picture, which is placed in the lower level of the temple, calls for far more pieces of antique glass than its companion art-glass skylight, which is positioned in one of the upper rooms in the temple. The baptistry window is made up of more than 3,000 pieces of glass.

Left: Tom Holdman, artist and master craftsman of the art glass to be used in the rebuilt Nauvoo Temple, is shown here working on the baptistry window. The creation of art-glass windows requires careful planning, patience, and skill as well as artistic talent. Holdman works with handblown glass from studios in Europe that specialize in the fashioning of antique glass.

LOR-

ASK UTAH ARTIST TOM HOLDMAN how long it took him to complete the two art-glass windows in the Nauvoo Temple and his answer is quick and telling: "All my life." These are not his first contributions to an LDS temple. He crafted the much-acclaimed windows in the LDS Palmyra Temple and the one at Winter Quarters. In each case, he began his work by "going to the temple." The imagery has come to him, he states, "by inspiration and direction from the Lord," a process he affirms is inherent in the building of temples. President Hinckley made the final decision for him to proceed on his designs.

"In the scriptures we read of the earth being transformed into its perfect state—'a sea of glass.' What better way to show that perfection in the temple than to use glass," he states.

Holdman has completed an interior window for the baptistry in the basement, a scene depicting the baptism of Jesus Christ by John the Baptist at the River Jordan. Of that work Holdman is clear. "It's the best thing I've ever done in my life." The other window is a skylight for the celestial room on an upper floor in the temple. This one is a blend of fifteen colors of glass in a complex design. The original temple also included a skylight in that room.

These windows, Holdman hopes, are more than just artistic imagery. He hopes each one communicates a feeling, a connection to the religious community it represents. The skylight interprets in brushed crystal the sacrifice of the Saints, he explains. "I used it to reminds us how the Saints in Kirtland smashed their china and crystal to give light to the walls of that early temple." He also put "links in the design to represent hooking together all ancestry in a chain."

What is most satisfying to him about his work? What is his favorite part of the process? "After it's done," Holdman explains, "I hold it up to the light and see how all the light falls and the window comes alive. After the hours and hours, I am never quite sure what it's going to look like. Then I hold it up and it catches the light." It's a singular moment for this artist whose life's work is illuminated before him.

ple are reinforced steel with a thick limestone veneer. The materials are representative of the worldwide reach of today's Church of Jesus Christ of Latter-day Saints. The stones came from a quarry in Alabama, were cut in Idaho, and finished in Salt Lake; the stone carvers came from Canada, the handblown glass from France, the wood flooring from Indonesia, the paint from Holland, the stained glass from Utah, and the bronze bell for the tower was cast in the Netherlands. The 7 exterior doors and 126 of the 138 windows, distinctive features of the Nauvoo Temple—then and now—were crafted just up the street from the temple by the recognized experts in historic restoration of window

Above: The furnishings in the reconstructed Temple reflect the fine workmanship that would have been used in such a splendid building in the mid-nineteenth century.

sashes and doors. States Charles W. Allen who heads up the family operation, "We've been blessed to have our abilities and talents extended far beyond our normal capabilities."

In harmony with how the early Saints built the first temple, three seasoned and experienced contractors, Okland Construction Company, Inc.; Layton Construction Company, Inc.; and Jacobsen Construction Company, Inc. joined together under the banner "Legacy Constructors" rather than compete for the sole honor of building this extraordinary temple themselves.

And while the early builders took on a project far beyond their capacity, the rebuilding has been characterized by ingenuity as well as zeal. Electrical and plumbing fixtures, air conditioning and heating conduits, and audio-visual equipment have been fitted into a structure initially designed with no thought for such amenities. The first Nauvoo Temple was a skeleton in comparison to the finished facility that is expected to draw LDS patrons from around the world.

Much of the construction process was a far cry from that of the early Saints: i.e. hard hats, giant hydraulic cranes, trucks, fork lifts, jackhammers, power drills, and computer imaging. Still, the parallels of the two building projects were dramatic. Both were characterized by long, hard days. Wind, rain, heat, cold—mud and mosquitoes—backdropped the six-day work weeks. In every aspect, then and now, there are accounts of miracles—from finding the original plans, to discovering the carved pattern on the stone buried beneath years of use on the original site, to crafting the windows.

Only a couple of photographs exist of the original building; none give a view of all sides of the temple. For the architects, reconstruction was boosted by access to the original William Weeks plans, which had been given to the Church in an unusual turn of events. Vern Thacker, an LDS missionary in the California Mission in 1946, came across the William Weeks architectural plans:

> "While we were tracting on the outskirts of town one day, we both felt inspired to stop at a small home. A man named Leslie M. Griffin invited us in and told us that he was a descendant of William Weeks, the architect for the Nauvoo LDS Temple." The missionar-

Joseph Smith solicited designs for the Nauvoo Temple and from the submissions he selected as architect William Weeks, a convert from the southern states. Weeks's initial design was a classic pedimented Greek temple with pilasters instead of columns surmounted by a tall Georgian tower. He drafted numerous sketches and drawings of the temple before the final composition and features were accepted by Joseph Smith. While some press accounts suggested the architecture was uniquely "the Mormon order," others classified the monumental structure facing west as "principally after the Roman style of architecture, somewhat intermixed with Grecian and Egyptian." Joseph Smith directed the whole temple building effort with the help of a committee—Alpheus Cutler, Reynolds Cahoon and Elias Higbee—who supervised the laborers, and Weeks who kept a close watch on the day-to-day construction. Visitor Josiah Quincy said of the temple's appearance, "it certainly cannot be compared to any ecclesiastical building." Shown here are sketches by William Weeks, as well as a detail of the ornamentation in the Assembly Hall in the reconstructed Nauvoo Temple based on these sketches.

Drawn by Wm Weeks   Nauvoo

ies visited him several times to discuss the gospel. Nearing the end of his mission, Elder Thacker made one last visit to Mr. Griffin who "excused himself for a few minutes and went into the back part of his house. He soon returned with a roll of what looked like poster paper about three feet long, ten inches in diameter, and secured with a rubber band. He explained that these were the original plans for the Nauvoo Temple and that they had been handed down in his family from his grandfather, William Weeks. He opened the bundle and showed the plans to us. The largest of the papers was a side view of the Temple exterior. Rolled inside of this piece were several other smaller drawings showing various views of the Temple." He asked Elder Thacker if on his way home he would carry "these plans to the headquarters of the Church in Salt Lake." The plans were delivered to the Church Historian's Office 28 September 1948, photographed and secured in "a steel-locked safe."[8]

The Nauvoo Temple walls today are one-foot-thick reinforced concrete faced with limestone veneer. The original walls were 18-inch-thick blocks of limestone. The stone quarries used for the original structure are no longer accessible—two are under water since the rise of the Mississippi from dams down river built in the early 1900s. The lime-

stone, just about a perfect match to the original right down to the black veins running through it, comes from a quarry near Russelville, Alabama, according to Keith P. MacKay who supervised the stonework. Stone carvers worked from fiberglass models created from photographs and pieces of stone. Ronald Prince is philosophical about each stage of the construction and the materials being used. "Each stone with its veining has a story of its own," he says. In his three years with the project he came to value, each "story" whether in the materials or the exactness, effort, commitment, and sacrifice of the workers. He emphasizes, "The key is what the temple is really for."

The surface finish of the blocks was discovered when, during excavation of the site, workers unearthed two stones, one with a distinctive "basket-weave" pattern and the other exhibiting a vertical striation—a parallel string of minute grooves—

Above: This basketweave pattern carved in the original temple stones was replicated on the massive stones of the modern structure. Stones uncovered on the temple site during excavation revealed the design making it possible for today's exterior to closely replicate the original finishing.

Top Left: A limestone fragment from the original temple shows the distinctive "ax-hammer strike," which is visible on the rebuilt structure.

Opposite: A spiral staircase of poured concrete sits in the southwest corner of the temple looping from the basement to the fifth floor. The first temple had similar stairs made of wood in three of the four corners of the temple.

called "ax-hammer strike." The stone, accurately carved by custom-fashioned chisels and hammers, authentically replicates the texture and design of the original building. Also uncovered in the roots of a tree was a star stone in fine condition.

Inside, the southwest free-standing circular staircase replicates in poured concrete what the Saints built with pine. The main-floor Assembly room stretches through the center of the building and rises, as did the original, through the second floor. The floors are wood, as were their predecessors, with area rugs to soften footsteps in the building. Offices, special endowment rooms,

"I HOPE WE HAVE DONE OUR WORK WELL ENOUGH THAT WE'VE GOT IT RIGHT."

—*Richard Holbrook, Legacy Construction Project Superintendent*

and sealing rooms are arranged to fit the needs of a working temple today. The celestial room on the third floor rises through the fourth floor and is crowned with an exquisite chandelier. A recreated Venetian-style window—approximately 22 feet wide—on the gabled east end echoes the grandeur of the earlier room.

In spite of the machinery and the construction know-how, those who worked on the site spoke with reverence of their task. "Sometimes

Left: The skylight of the celestial room catches the brilliance of the sun as if to say, "Stand still, and consider the wondrous works of God."

O N FEB. 6, 2001, THREE WALL MURALS WERE HUNG on the third floor of the Nauvoo LDS temple. For the next week, the team of six artists put their finishing touches on work which had been an eighteen-month odyssey. It had been, for them, the journey of a lifetime.

The work began with Frank Magleby's mission to paint original paintings for the temples in England, the United States, and South America. At the conclusion of that assignment, the temple department approached him to assemble a small group of artists to provide paintings, perhaps murals, for the Nauvoo Temple. The Los Angeles Temple, completed in 1956, was the last LDS Temple where murals were included in the interior design.

Each of the artists was encouraged to bring his own style to the work. "They didn't want six artists in a blender," James Christensen explains. The assignment was expected to last three to four months. It became consuming not just for them but for their families

Far Above: Doug Fryer and his family moved from Vermont and lived with relatives while he and Robert Marshall painted a mural featuring scenes from the first chapters of Genesis.

Above: The artists painted the canvases in the Motion Picture Studio in Provo, Utah, where they had designed the lighting to replicate the lighting in the Nauvoo Temple. The canvases were then adhered to the walls of the temple and the artists filled in the corners and did their final touches. Frank Magelby stated that when they hung the paintings on the wall, it was like "taking a picture and putting it in a frame. [The murals] take on a special presence when you see [them] go up on the wall."

Left: Gary Smith filling in the corner on a mural. Smith and Magleby joined together to paint a landscape in the style of the grand scenery painters of the Hudson River School.

who were enlisted to help with sketching and to put down base color. The artists worked in pairs and visited different parts of the country taking pictures and sketching ideas for the massive landscapes. Scaffolding, lights, canvas, and paint took over a whole portion of what was usually a setting for making films. None of the artists had ever painted anything so big.

The artists crafted an architectural model showing the murals in place so that those giving final approval could place the paintings in perspective. Once approval was given, the artists went to work. Gary Smith sketched his images on the canvas freehand with bold charcoal strokes. Chris Young used a shaded pencil to create the composition for the whole wall he and Christensen would complete, then projected it up for painting.

Some methodically worked right to left; others worked on first one part of the wall, then another. Frank Magleby and Gary Smith were the first finished.

The murals were completed by the first week in December. The canvases were then rolled up and trucked to Illinois for placement in the temple. The artists spent a week putting finishing touches on the murals in their intended setting.

"When we came around the bend into Nauvoo at night, all the lights were on in the temple," recalls James Christensen. "For the first time, I was seeing what the early Saints had built and it surpassed all expectations, not just mine, but all six of us were deeply touched. The day we finished our work, we came back in the evening and offered our work to the Lord in prayer."

Above Left: Lead Artist Frank Magleby brought to-gether the artistic team of six to design and paint the three murals for rooms on the third floor of the temple.

Above: James Christensen underpainting a section of the mural. Christensen and Young visited locations and took photographs rich in foliage to help them visualize their images for canvas.

Above: Robert Marshall works on one of the murals. "So much of what happens in a mural happens while you paint it," he contends "We are not doing these to decorate a space, we are not doing them to demonstrate our own prowess or ability. We want the work to feel appropriate for where it is, to elevate." Chris Young adds that the murals contribute to "a calm kind of feeling—peace, harmony. I hope the murals blend with the whole artistic statement [of the temple] from the furniture to the stonework."

Above: Chris Young and James Christensen discuss final touches after the canvas has been adhered to the walls of the temple.

Left. The charge to artists Gary Smith, Doug Fryer, Robert Marshall, James Christensen, Frank Magleby, and Chris Young was to paint scenes that would "fit in the 1840s." The artists had worked together on other projects so they were comfortable offering advice to one another. Frank Magleby speaks for all six artists when he says, "The murals are the most important thing I have ever done. I feel like this is [an] opportunity that comes along once in a lifetime.

Creating on Canvas

at night I walk through the temple," reflects Richard Holbrook, Legacy Construction Project Superintendent, "it's late, it's dark and I realize what a responsibility this is."

The completed temple will sit amidst red oak trees, wrought-iron fencing, manicured lawns, and gardens more reminiscent of current LDS temple settings than early Nauvoo. No effort was made in the winding-up days of temple construction in 1845 to beautify the grounds. A newly constructed parking garage across Mulholland introduces a practical touch of the twenty-first century to the historic location.

Touring the temple after the Saints had fled Nauvoo, a reporter for the *Palmyra Courier-Journal*, the locale of the Church's beginnings, called the temple "the most conspicuous object, in fact the only conspicuous object in the city." That distinction holds today.

The Nauvoo Temple stands again in its place as the centerpiece of old Nauvoo. But it is more than a landmark. It is a statement of a people "whose God is the Lord." These nineteenth-century Saints chose God because they believed He chose them. Said Sarah Rich, "We had faith in our Heavenly Father, and we put our trust in Him, feeling that we were His chosen people and had embraced His gospel."[9]

The Nauvoo temple shaped a tradition—above its entrance, and on all LDS temples around the world, (presently more than one hundred), is the message, *Holiness to the Lord*. These gilt letters speak both tribute and testimony. They are the essence of belief that sustained a people bludgeoned by public opinion and even mob violence, yet a people resolute and resilient. Their efforts at building a community had little to do with land and everything to do with the tradition of the ancients to build a house for God. It was His community that they sought in His house. The temple's legacy of sacrifice, courage, faith, resilience, and devotion is not lost on this polished new structure. It, too, speaks of a cause born within, a cause shaped by sacred purpose—within walls of sacred stone.

Far Above: The baptismal font (shown under construction) was designed to match its predecessor. The oval font then was sixteen feet long, twelve feet wide, and four feet deep. The rim stood seven feet above the floor. Water for the font was drawn from a thirty-foot well dug in the Temple basement's east end. The lower level then—and now—is paved with bricks in a pattern that converges at the font in the center of the room.

Above: The Temple Assembly Hall on the main floor under construction. It was in the original Assembly Hall on 5 October 1845 that the Saints sustained the decision of Church authorities to abandon the temple and Nauvoo and flee west in the spring.

Opposite: The regal furnishings of the Celestial Room add to the room's majesty.

AUTHORITIES CITED

Following are the names and professional affiliations or positions of those people interviewed in connection with the documentary SACRED STONE: TEMPLE ON THE MISSISSIPPI, *who are quoted in this companion book,* SACRED STONE: THE TEMPLE AT NAUVOO. *Quotations that appear in this volume were all selected from transcripts of these interviews.*

DR. RICHARD E. AHLBORN
Curator, Smithsonian Museum of
History, Washington, D.C.
Interviewed August 28, 2001.

DR. JOHN BUTLER
Historian, American Studies, Yale
University, Connecticut
Interviewed August 29, 2001.

DR. RODNEY O. DAVIS
Co-director, Lincoln Studies Center,
Knox College, Illinois
Interviewed May 23, 2001.

DR. GLEN M. LEONARD
Curator, Museum of Church History and
Art, The Church of Jesus Christ of Latter-
day Saints, Salt Lake City, Utah
Interviewed February 23, 2001.

DR. EDWIN S. GAUSTAD
Professor Emeritus, University of
California at Riverside
Interviewed May 30, 2001.

PRESIDENT GORDON B. HINCKLEY
The Church of Jesus Christ of Latter-day
Saints, Headquarters in Salt Lake City, Utah
Interviewed May 30, 2001.

DR. LOREN N. HORTON
Senior Historian,
State Historical Society of Iowa
Interviewed May 23, 2001.

DR. JOHN M. LUNDQUIST
The Susan and Douglas Dillon Chief
Librarian, Asian and Middle Eastern
Division, The New York Public Library
Interviewed August 31, 2001.

DR. TRUMAN G. MADSEN
Professor Emeritus; Former Director,
Jerusalem Center for Near Eastern
Studies, Brigham Young University, Utah
Interviewed February 23, 2001.

DR. CAROL MEYERS
Biblical Studies and Archaeology, Duke
University, North Carolina
Interviewed August 28, 2001.

DR. RUSSELL M. NELSON
Quorum of the Twelve Apostles
The Church of Jesus Christ of Latter-day
Saints, Headquarters in Utah
Interviewed November 28, 2001.

DR. JACOB NEUSNER
Religion and Theology, Bard College,
New York
Interviewed August 30, 2001.

MAYOR CHARLES W. SCHOLZ
Quincy, Illinois
Interviewed May 24, 2001.

ENDNOTES

PREFACE

1. William Clayton, "Journal Three, Nauvoo Temple 1845-1846," in *An Intimate Chronicle: The Journals of William Clayton*, ed. George D. Smith (Salt Lake City: Signature Books, 1995), 225.

2. Ibid., 532.

3. Sarah Dearmon Pea Rich, Autobiography 1814–1893, typescript, L. Tom Perry Special Collections, Harold B. Lee Library, Brigham Young University, p. 42.

4. Clayton, *An Intimate Chronicle*, 221.

5. Joseph Kingsbury, Autobiography, typescript, Historical Department Archives, The Church of Jesus Christ of Latter-day Saints, p. 3.

INTRODUCTION

1. Thomas L. Kane. Quoted by George A. Smith, in *Journal of Discourses*, 13:114–118.

CHAPTER 1: FROM ANCIENT DAYS

1. Joseph Smith, *The Words of Joseph Smith: The Contemporary Accounts of the Nauvoo Discourses of the Prophet Joseph*, compiled and edited by Andrew F. Ehat and Lyndon W. Cook (Provo: BYU Religious Studies Center, 1980), 418.

2. Theodore Parker, quoted in Hyrum L. Andrus, *Doctrinal Themes of the Doctrine and Covenants* (Provo: Brigham Young University Press, 1964), 12.

3. Ralph Waldo Emerson, Ibid, 11.

4. Joseph Smith Jr., *History of the Church of Jesus Christ of Latter-day Saints*, ed. B. H. Roberts (Salt Lake City: Deseret Book Co., 1965), 4:449.

5. Ibid, 4:661.

6. Frederic G. Mather, "The Early Days of Mormonism," *Lippincott's Magazine* 26 (August 1880): 208. Quoted in Elwin Clark Robison, *The First Mormon Temple: Design, Construction, and Historic Context of the Kirtland Temple* (Provo: Brigham Young University Press, 1997), 188.

Above: Carving on a door frame reflects the attention to detail in every aspect of the temple.

7. Lucy Mack Smith, *History of Joseph Smith by His Mother* (Salt Lake City: Stevens & Wallis, Inc., 1945), 230.

8. *History of the Church*, 2:167.

9. Joseph Smith, *The Words of Joseph Smith*, 245.

10. *History of the Church*, 2:382.

11. Ibid., 2:428.

12. *Journal of Discourses*, 11:10.

13. Edward W. Tullidge, *The Women of Mormondom* (New York: Tullidge & Crandall, 1877), 95.

14. Carol Cornwall Madsen, ed., *In Their Own Words: Women and the Story of Nauvoo* (Salt Lake City: Deseret Book Co., 1994), 249.

15. Littlefield, Lyman O., *Reminiscences of Latter-day Saints*, (Logan, Utah: The Utah Journal Co., 1888), 72–73.

16. Joseph Smith, quoted in J. Earl Arrington "William Weeks, Architect of the Nauvoo Temple," *BYU Studies* 19, no. 3 (Spring 1979): 347.

17. Perrigrine Sessions, "Journal," 30 January 1846, Historical Department Archives, The Church of Jesus Christ of Latter-day Saints.

18. J.M. Davidson, quoted in E. Cecil McGavin, *The Nauvoo Temple* (Salt Lake City: Deseret Book Co., 1962), 93.

CHAPTER 2: BUILDING THE KINGDOM

1. *History of the Church*, 6:230.

2. *Quincy Whig*, 22 December 1838.

3. *History of the Church*, 4:338–339.

4. Hyrum L. Andrus and Helen Mae Andrus, comps., *They Knew the Prophet* (Salt Lake City: Bookcraft, 1974), 71.

5. C. Madsen, ed., *In their Own Words*, 250.

6. *Quincy Whig, 2 March, 1839*.

7. *History of the Church*, 4:339.

Above: "Mormon History in the Making" Photo taken on February 4, 2002—the 156th anniversary of the Exodus down the Trail of Hope, capturing the view the early Saints beheld as they left Nauvoo.

8. Richard E. Bennett, *We'll Find the Place* (Salt Lake City: Deseret Book Co., 1997), xv; Taine's "Essay on the Mormons," trans. Austin E. Fife, in *Pacific Historical Review* 31, no.1 (Feb. 1962), 60.

9. Eliza R. Snow, "Sketch of My Life," 12.

10. *History of the Church*, 4:610.

11. *Pittsburgh Gazette*, 3 December, 1843.

12. John Pulsipher, Diary. Quoted in N.B. Lundwall, *Temples of the Most High* (Salt Lake City: Bookcraft, 1968), 52–53.

13. William Adams, Autobiography, typescript, Special Collections, Harold B. Lee Library, Brigham Young University, p. 11.

14. Josiah Quincy, "Joseph Smith Recollections by Josiah Quincy, Figures of the Past," in *Writings of Early Latter-day Saints,* Milton V. Backman, Jr., comp. in cooperation with Keith W. Perkins (Provo: Religious Studies Center, 1996), 389.

15. Ibid.

16. Leonard J. Arrington, "Mormonism: Views from Without and Within," *BYU Studies* 14, no. 2 (Winter 1974): 153.

17. *Journal of Discourses*, 2:32.

CHAPTER 3: NO MATTER THE SACRIFICE

1. Autobiography of James Leithead. In family's possession.

2. Caroline Crosby, Journal, Historical Department Archives, The Church of Jesus Christ of Latter-day Saints. Quoted in Kenneth W. Godfrey, "Some Thoughts Regarding an Unwritten History of Nauvoo," *BYU Studies* 15, no. 4 (Summer 1975): 419.

3. Wilford Woodruff, *Leaves from My Journal* (Salt Lake City: Juvenile Instructor Office, 1881), 75.

4. *History of the Church*, 4:186.

5. Ibid.

6. Christopher Layton. Quoted in Richard L. Jensen, "Transplanted to Zion: The Impact of British Latter-day Saint Immigration Upon Nauvoo," *BYU Studies* 31, no. 1 (Winter 1991): 79.

7. Louisa Decker, "Reminiscences of Nauvoo," *Woman's Exponent* 37 (March 1909) 41.

8. Mervin L. Gifford, "Stephen Markham: Man of Valour" (Master's Thesis, Brigham Young University, 1973).

9. *New York Herald*, 19 January 1842. Cited in Roy W. Doxey, *The Doctrine and Covenants Speaks* (Salt Lake City: Deseret Book Co., 1964), 2:452.

10. *St. Louis Republican*, Saturday, 1 June 1844.

11. *History of the Church*, 6:196–97.

12. *Illinois State Register*, 31 March 1843, p. 1. Quoted in Hyrum L. Andrus, *Joseph Smith, the Man and the Seer* (Salt Lake City: Deseret Book Co., 1960), 106.

13. William Allred, Autobiography, copy of holograph, Historical Department Archives, The Church of Jesus Christ of Latter-day Saints, 7–8.

14. Joseph Holbrook, Autobiography, typescript, Harold B. Lee Library, Brigham Young University, Special Collections, p. 58.

15. *Times and Seasons*, 15 April 1841.

16. *History of the Church*, 4:329.

17. Norton Jacobs, Autobiography, Special Collections, Harold B. Lee Library, Brigham Young University, *Writings of Early Latter-day Saints*, 6.

18. *Warsaw Signal*, 19 May 1841.

19. Wandle Mace, Autobiography, Special Collections, Harold B. Lee Library, Brigham Young University.

20. Nancy Tracy, Autobiography, typescript, Special Collections, Harold B. Lee Library, Brigham Young University, p. 26.

21. *History of the Church*, 4:517.

22. Ibid, 6:243.

23. William Clayton, "An Interesting Journal," *Juvenile Instructor* 21 (15 January–15 October 1886).

24. "'All Things Move in Order in the City': The Nauvoo Diary of Zina Diantha Huntington Jacobs," Maureen Ursenbach Beecher, ed., *BYU Studies* 19, no. 3 (Spring 1979).

25. James M. Adams to Joseph Smith, 16 November 1842, Whitney Collection, Brigham Young University. Quoted in Donna Hill, *Joseph Smith: The First Mormon* (New York: Doubleday & Company, Inc., 1977), 294–295.

26. Matilda Loveless, Autobiography, typescript, Special Collections, Harold B. Lee Library, Brigham Young University, p. 1.

27. Carol Cornwall Madsen, "Mormon Women and the Temple: Toward a New Understanding," in *Sisters in Spirit* (Urbana and Chicago: University of Illinois Press, 1987), 83.

28. "'All Things Move in Order in the City': The Nauvoo Diary of Zina Diantha Huntington Jacobs," Maureen Ursenbach Beecher, ed., *BYU Studies* 19, no. 3 (Spring 1979).

CHAPTER 4: THE FIRE OF ISRAEL'S GOD

1. Jane Robinson, quoted in Richard Neitzel Holzapfel and Jeni Brober Holzapfel, *Women of Nauvoo* (Salt Lake City: Bookcraft, 1992), 15–16.

2. Orson F. Whitney, *Life of Heber C. Kimball* (Salt Lake City: Kimball Family, 1888), 265–266.

3. Brigham Young and Willard Richards letter to First Presidency, 5 September1840. Quoted in Susan Evans McCloud, *Brigham Young, A Personal Portrait* (American Fork, UT: Covenant Communications, 1996), 95–96.

4. *Millennial Star* 1, no. 1 (May 1840).

5. "Cold Comfort," *Times and Seasons* 3, no. 24 (October 14, 1842), 954.

6. Ronald W. Walker, "Cradling Mormonism: The Rise of the Gospel in Early Victorian England," *BYU Studies* 27, no. 1 (Winter1987), 31.

7. *History of the Church*, 4:127.

8. Wilford Woodruff to Willard Richards, 31 March 1840. Quoted in James B. Allen and Malcom R. Thorp, "The Mission of the Twelve to England, 1840–41: Mormon Apostles and the Working Classes," *BYU Studies* 15, no. 4 (Summer 1975), 505.

9. Elden Jay Watson, ed., *Manuscript History of Brigham Young*, 1801–1844, (Salt Lake City: Elden Jay Watson, 1968), 97. Quoted in Stanley B. Kimball, "Heber C. Kimball and Family, the Nauvoo Years," *BYU Studies* 15, no. 4 (Summer 1975): 450.

10. Leonard J. Arrington and Davis Bitton, *The Mormon Experience* (Urbana and Chicago: University of Illinois Press, 1992), 68.

11. *Millennial Star* 1: 252–255.

12. *Millennial Star* 1: 263, February 1841; 2:96, October 1841.

13. Alexander Neibaur Journal, 1841, in possession of Dr. Jeff O'Driscoll. Spelling and punctuation corrected.

14. Madelyn Player, *The Legacy of William Warner Player* 1793–1993 (Salt Lake City: Publishers Press, 1993), 19.

15. William Clayton letter, 10 December 1840 (Historical Department Archives, The Church of Jesus Christ of Latter-day Saints). Quoted in Heidi S. Swinton, *Pioneer Spirit: Modern-Day Stories of Courage and Conviction* (Salt Lake City: Deseret Book Co., 1996), 8.

16. *Millennial Star*, 4:89 (October 1843).

17. Quoted in Arrington and Bitton, *Mormon Experience*, 71.

18. Player, *The Legacy of William Warner Player*, 21.

19. William Clayton, "An Interesting Journal," *Juvenile Instructor* 21 (15 January–15 October 1886).

20. Charles Lambert, Autobiography, typescript, Special Collections, Harold B. Lee Library, Brigham Young University, p. 13.

21. *History of the Church*, 4:609.

22. Ibid., 6:298.

23. Ibid., 5:23-25.

24. Jill Mulvay Derr, Janath Russell Cannon, and Maureen Ursenbach Beecher, *Women of Covenant: The Story of Relief Society* (Salt Lake City: Deseret Book Co., 1992), 34.

25. Ibid., 51.

26. *History of the Church*, 6:143.

27. Louisa Barnes Pratt, "Autobiography," 232.

28. *History of the Church*, 6:298–299.

29. Donald C. Colvin, "A Historical Study of the Mormon Temple at Nauvoo, Illinois," section IV (Master's Thesis, Brigham Young University, August 1962).

30. Smith, *The Words of Joseph Smith*, 164–168.

31. *History of the Church*, 4:212–213.

32. Ibid., 4:492–493.

33. "'They Might Have Known That He Was Not a Fallen Prophet'–The Nauvoo Journal of Joseph Fielding," Andrew F. Ehat, ed. and transcriber, *BYU Studies* 19, no. 2 (Winter 1979): 141.

34. Ibid.

35. *Alton Telegraph*, 14 November 1840.

36. *New York Sun*, 4 September 1843. Quoted in Arrington and Bitton, *The Mormon Experience*, 65.

37. Ibid.

38. Smith, *The Words of Joseph Smith*, 418.

Chapter 5: Holy Work

1. Heber C. Kimball to Parley P. Pratt, 17 June 1842, Parley P. Pratt papers, Ca. Quoted in Richard O. Cowan, *Temples to Dot the Earth* (Salt Lake City: Deseret Book Co., 1993), 54.

2. Josiah Quincy, *Figures of the Past*, 386 ff.

3. *Teachings of the Prophet Joseph Smith*, 20 March 1842, 197–98.

4. William Clayton, "An Interesting Journal," *Juvenile Instructor* 21 (15 January–15 October, 1886), 2-20; 23-311).

5. *Teachings of the Prophet Joseph Smith*, 197–98.

6. *History of the Church*, 7:323.

7. *Times and Seasons*, Monday, 1 January 1844.

8. *History of the Church*, 4:269.

9. Ibid., 4:187.

10. Daniel H. Wells. Quoted in Hyrum L. Andrus, *Joseph Smith*, 56.

11. *History of the Church*, 4:568-569.

12. Ibid., 4:377-378.

13. Wilford Woodruff, Excerpt from Sermon delivered at the General Conference 6 April 1891. Quoted in Lundwall, *Temples of the Most High*, 69.

14. E. Cecil McGavin, *The Nauvoo Temple*, 10.

15. Ibid., 51.

16. Wilford Woodruff. Quoted in John A. Widtsoe, *Joseph Smith–Seeker after Truth, Prophet of God*, (Salt Lake City: Bookcraft, 1951), 308.

17. *Times and Seasons*, 15 September, 651.

18. Lucius N. Scovil, letter to the editor, *Deseret News*, Semi-Weekly, 15 February 1884, 2.

19. James Henry Rollins. Quoted in Andrus and Andrus, *They Knew the Prophet*, 77.

20. Franklin D. Richards, *Contributor* 7, no. 8 (May 1886): 301.

21. Joseph Fielding, "The Nauvoo Journal," 22-23.

22. Mercy Fielding Thompson, "Recollections of the Prophet Joseph Smith," *The Juvenile Instructor 27* (1 July 1892), 400.

23. Diary of Bathsheba Wilson Bigler Smith, in the author's possession.

24. Parley P. Pratt, *Autobiography of Parley P. Pratt*, ed. Parley P. Pratt, Jr. (Salt Lake City: Deseret Book Co., 1985), 259–260.

25. Wandle Mace, Autobiography, typescript, Special Collections, Harold B. Lee Library, Brigham Young University, p. 195.

26. Joseph Smith. Quoted in Parley P. Pratt, "Proclamation,"*Millennial Star* 5, no. 10 (March 1845): 151.

Chapter 6: Citizenry on Edge

1. *History of the Church*, 6:497.

2. Harvey Cluff, Autobiography, typescript, Special Collections, Harold B. Lee Library, Brigham Young University, p. 4–5.

3. Thomas Ford, History of Illinois, 348: as quoted in "From Assassination to Expulsion: Two Years of Distrust, Hostility, and Violence" by Marshall Hamilton Fn, *BYU Studies*, vol. 32 (1992), nos. 1 and 2 (Winter and Spring, 1992).

4. John E. Hallwas, "Nauvoo from a Non-Mormon Perspective," in *Kingdom on the Mississippi Revisited*, eds. Roger D. Launius and John E. Hallwas (Urbana and Chicago: University of Illinois Press, 1996), 1.

5. Marshall Hamilton, "From Assassination To Expulsion: Two Years of Distrust, Hostility, and

Violence," *BYU Studies* 32, no. 1 and 2 (Winter and Spring 1992): 245.

6. *History of the Church*, 7:281.

7. Letter of John Nevius, 2 May 1841, Stanley Kimball Collection, Southern Illinois University. Quoted in Hill, *Joseph Smith*, 286.

8. *History of the Church*, 7:361.

9. Ibid., 4:231.

10. George Givens, *In Old Nauvoo: Everyday Life in the City of Joseph* (Salt Lake City: Deseret Book Co., 1993), 135.

11. "Letter from an Englishman," *Millennial Star* 4, no.10 (February 1844): 153.

12. "Mormonism," *Times and Seasons* 3, no. 16 (15 June 1842): 829.

13. "Letter from an Englishman," 153.

14. *History of the Church*, 7:3.

15. Hamilton, "From Assassination to Expulsion," 229.

16. *Journal of Discourses*, 13:348.

17. Ibid., 3:266.

18. Ehat and Cook, *Words of Joseph Smith*, 209-212.

19. Hallwas, "Nauvoo from a Non-Mormon Perspective," 169.

20. Ibid, 171.

21. Ibid, 171.

22. *History of the Church*, 2:230.

23. Eliza R. Snow, *Biography and Family Record of Lorenzo Snow* (Salt Lake City: Deseret News, 1884), 393–394.

24. Jerry C. Jolley, "The Sting of the Wasp: Early Nauvoo Newspapers, April 1842–April 1843, *BYU Studies*, 22 (1982) no. 4 (Fall 1982).

25. *History of the Church*, 2:85.

26. Charles A. Foster, *Warsaw Signal*, 12 June 1844.

27. *History of the Church*, 6:496.

28. Arrington and Bitton, *Mormon Experience*, 78.

29. *History of the Church*, 6:498.

30. Ibid., 6:554.

31. Quoted in Dallin H. Oaks and Marvin S. Hill, *Carthage Conspiracy* (Urbana and Chicago: University of Illinois Press, 1979), 19.

32. John Pulsipher Diary

33. *History of the Church*, 6:624–625.

34. Clayton, "An Interesting Journal," in *Juvenile Instructor* 21 (Jan. 15-Oct. 15, 1886), 2-20; 231-311.

35. Richard E. Bennett, *We'll Find the Place* (Salt Lake City: Deseret Book Co., 1997), 1.

36. Vilate Kimball to Heber C. Kimball, 30 June 1844. Quoted in Davis Bitton, *The Martyrdom Remembered* (Salt Lake City: Aspen Books, 1994), 7.

37. "Joseph Smith, the Prophet," *Young Woman's Journal* 16 (December 1905): 554.

38. William Hyde, Journal, Historical Department Archives, The Church of Jesus Christ of Latter-day Saints.

39. *Times and Seasons*, quoted in McGavin, *The Nauvoo Temple*, 50.

40. Clayton, "An Interesting Journal."

CHAPTER 7: THE LAST STONES

1. Maureen Ursenbach Beecher, ed., "'All Things Move in Order in the City': The Nauvoo Diary of Zina Diantha Huntington Jacobs."

2. Lewis van Buren to James J. Strang, 14 March 1846. Quoted in Bennett, *We'll Find the Place*, 14.

3. C. Madsen, *In Their Own Words*, 254.

4. *History of the Church*, 7:254–256.

5. Ibid., 7:234.

6. *Deseret Evening News*, 12 March 1892.

7. Lynne Watkins Jorgensen, "The Mantle of the Prophet Joseph Passes to Brother Brigham: A Collective Spiritual Witness," *BYU Studies* 36, no. 4 (1996–1997).

8. Ibid.

9. Ibid.

10. Player, *The Legacy of William Warner Player*, 86.

11. Susan Easton Black, *Who's Who in the Doctrine and Covenants* (Salt Lake City: Bookcraft, 1997), 225–226.

12. Arza Adams, Journal, 15 August 1827–18 February 1901, Special Collections, Harold B. Lee Library, Brigham Young University, 20 November 1844.

13. Quoted in Arrington and Bitton, *The Mormon Experience*, 85.

14. Quoted in Ronald K. Esplin, "Reorganization Began New Church Era," *Church News*, 20 December 1997.

15. Journal History, 17 March 1845.

16. Irene Hascall to her parents, 6 and 26 July 1845. Quoted in Bennett, *We'll Find the Place*, 20.

17. Tracy, Autobiography, 25–26.

18. Joseph Grafton Hovey biography. In possession of his family.

19. Elizabeth Heard, autobiography in Parkhill Terry Family History (1956), 70.

20. Leonard J. Arrington, Brigham Young: American Moses (New York: Alfred Knopf, 1985), 123.

21. *History of the Church*, 2:472.

22. Clayton, "An Interesting Journal."

23. *History of the Church*, 7:357.

24. Clayton, "An Interesting Journal."

25. *Journal of Discourses*, 1:133.

26. Joseph Fielding, "The Nauvoo Journal," 158–159.

27. Helen Mar Whitney, *A Woman's View: Helen Mar Whitney's Reminiscences of Early Church History* (Provo: BYU Religious Studies Center, 1999), 262–263.

28. *History of the Church*, 7:417–418.

29. Quoted in McGavin, *The Nauvoo Temple*, 36–37.

30. Ibid., 50.

31. Norton Jacobs, Autobiography, typescript, Special Collections, Harold B. Lee Library, Brigham Young University, p. 13–14.

32. William P. Richards, *Warsaw Signal*, 7 February, Historical Department Archives, The Church of Jesus Christ of Latter-day Saints (MS8829).

33. "The John Taylor Nauvoo Journal," *BYU Studies* 23, no. 2 (Spring1983).

34. George A. Smith, *Journal of Discourses*, 2:23.

35. Willard Richards. Quoted in Hamilton, "From Assassination To Expulsion," 230.

36. *History of the Church*, 7:240.

37. Jacob Peart, Autobiography, Historic Nauvoo Library and Research Center.

38. Loveless, Autobiography, 1.

39. George Whitaker, "Life of George Whitaker, A Pioneer," as written by himself, typescript, Utah State Historical Society. Quoted in Carol Cornwall Madsen, *Journey to Zion: Voices from the Mormon Trail* (Salt Lake City: Deseret Book Co., 1997), 50.

40. Bathsheba Smith, Autobiography, typescript, Special Collections, Harold B. Lee Library, Brigham Young University, p. 11.

41. *History of the Church*, 7:440.

42. Ibid., 7:430.

43. Smith, *The Words of Joseph Smith*, 417.

44. Millennial Star, vol. 6 (June 1845–December 1845), no. 11, 168.

45. *New York Messenger*, August 30, 1845.

46. *History of the Church*, 7: 430–431.

47. Ibid., 7:259.

48. *Quincy Whig*, 22 September 1845.

49. *Nauvoo Neighbor*, 1 October 1845.

50. Norton Jacobs, Autobiography, 14.

51. William Clayton, "An Interesting Journal," *Juvenile Instructor* 21 (15 January–15 October 1886).

52. *History of the Church*, 7:456.

53. Ibid., 7:456–457.

54. C. Madsen, *Journey to Zion*, 52–53.

55. "Foote, Warren," in Jenson, Andrew, ed., *Latter-day Saint Biographical Encyclopedia: A Compilation of Biographical Sketches of Prominent Men and Women in the Church of Jesus Christ of Latter-day Saints*, 4 vols. (Salt Lake City: A. Jenson History Company and Deseret News, 1901–36), 1:375.

56. *History of the Church*, 7:478.

CHAPTER 8: CITY FOR SALE

1. *Journal of Discourses,* 8:387; see also *Deseret News,* Vol. 2, 13 March 1861.

2. Mace, Autobiography, 186.

3. H. Whitney, *A Woman's View*, 313.

4. McGavin, *The Nauvoo Temple*, 64.

5. "All Things Move in Order in the City."

6. *History of the Church*, 7:536.

7. Lemuel Herrick & Sally Judd, Biography, HNL&R, p. 6.

8. Norton Jacobs, p.14.

9. John Pulsipher, Autobiography, typescript, Special Collections, Harold B. Lee Library, Brigham Young University, p. 8–9.

10. "The Life History of James Henry Rollins," unpublished, in author's possession, 15.

11. *History of the Church*, 7: 434–435.

12. Ibid., 4: 566.

13. Quoted in McGavin, *The Nauvoo Temple*, 27.

14. Quoted in Givens, *In Old Nauvoo*, 149–150.

15. The *Palmyra Courier Journal*, 22 September 1847. Quoted in McGavin, *The Nauvoo Temple*, 36.

16. Erastus Snow, "A Journal or Sketch of the Life of Erastus Snow," typescript, BYU, p. 19.

17. *History of the Church*, 7:567.

18. Elizabeth Ann Whitney, quoted in C. Madsen, *In Their Own Words*, 22.

19. *Quincy Rifleman* 1843-45, 30 September 1845.

20. Zina Diantha Huntington, quoted in C. Madsen, *In Their Own Words*, 86.

21. *Journal of Discourses*, 14:219.

22. Jacobs, Autobiography, p. 23.

23. Ibid., p. 30.

24. H. Whitney, *A Woman's View*, 327.

25. Zora Smith Jarvis, *Ancestry Biography and Family of George A. Smith* (Provo: Brigham Young University Press, 1962), 28.

26. *History of the Church*, 7:580.

27. Ibid., 7:579.

28. Ara Sabin, Autobiography, typescript, Historical Department Archives, The Church of Jesus Christ of Latter-day Saints, p. 3.

29. Eliza R. Snow, *Biography and Family Record of Lorenzo Snow*, 85.

30. James L. Blanchard to William Smith, 6 November 1846, Beinecke Library, Yale University. Quoted in Richard E. Bennett, "Battle of Nauvoo Was Final Chapter in the Expulsion From Beloved Zion," *Church News*, 14 September 1996.

31. Eliza R. Snow, *Biography and Family Record of Lorenzo Snow*, 159-160.

32. *Journal of Discourses*, 2:32.

33. James A. Little, *From Kirtland to Salt Lake City* (Salt Lake City: James A. Little, Publisher, 1890), 46.

34. Biography of Henry Grow, in the family's possession. *Quincy Whig* article is quoted in this source.

35. *Warsaw Signal*, 21 November 1846.

36. *Journal of Discourses*, 8:356.

37. *History of the Church*, 7:596.

38. Samuel Richards, Diary, typescript, Special Collections, Harold B. Lee Library, Brigham Young University, p. 19.

39. Wilford Woodruff, *Wilford Woodruff, His Life and Labors*, comp. Matthias F. Cowley (Salt Lake City: Deseret News, 1916) 248.

40. *History of the Church*, 7:596.

41. Robert Flanders, *Nauvoo: Kingdom on the Mississippi* (Urbana and Chicago: University of Illinois, 1975) 339.

42. *Journal of Discourses*, 2:23.

43. Ann Eliza Coffin Garner, Journal, in family's possession.

44. *Burlington Iowa Hawkeye*, 17 September 1846.

45. B.H. Roberts, *Contributor* 8, no. 12 (October 1887): 452.

46. Ann Eliza Coffin Garner, Journal.

47. Bennett, "Battle of Nauvoo"; Josiah B. Convers, "A Brief History of the Hancock Mob in the Year 1846" (St. Louis: Cathcart and Prescott, 1846) 17–21.

48. Sarah Rich, Autobiography, p. 42–43.

49. Brigham Young discourse, 2 January 1846. Quoted in H. Whitney, *A Woman's View*, 312–313..

50. Bennett, *We'll Find the Place*, 25.

51. Wandle Mace, Autobiography, p. 207.

52. The *Missouri Whig*, 21 May 1846.

53. McGavin, *The Nauvoo Temple*, 143.

54. *History of the Church*, 7:435.

55. McGavin, *The Nauvoo Temple*, 107.

56. Ibid., 146.

57. Ibid., 143.

58. *Journal of Discourses*, 10:253.

59. The *Carthage Republican*, 2 February 1865.

CHAPTER 9: COME AFTER US

1. Thomas L. Kane. Quoted in *Journal of Discourses*, 13:114–118.

2. Brigham Young discourse, 2 January 1846. Quoted in H. Whitney, *A Woman's View*, 312–313.

3. Arza Erastus Hinckley, Autobiography, p. 1.

4. Sabin, Autobiography, p. 3.

5. Gordon B. Hinckley, Cornerstone Ceremony, 5 November 2000, Nauvoo, Illinois.

6. Boyd K. Packer, Cornerstone Ceremony, 5 November 2000, Nauvoo, Illinois.

7. *Journal History*, 12 June 1844.

8. Vern C. Thacker, "The Nauvoo Temple Architect's Drawings Lost and Found," 20 January 2000. Used with permission.

9. Sarah Rich, Autobiography, p. 42–43.

PHOTOGRAPHS AND ARTWORK

Front Endsheet: Rendering of the city of Nauvoo from across the river, courtesy of Illinois State Historical Library, Old State Capitol Building, Springfield, IL 62701.

Page ii: Nauvoo Temple rendering, by Steven T. Baird ca. 1960, courtesy of Nauvoo Restoration, Inc.

Page vi: *The Home of the Saints in Illinois, The Rocky Mountain Saints: A Full and Complete History of the Mormons,* 1878, Ward, Lock, & Tyler, Warwick House, Paternoster Row, E.C.

Page vii: Mud-chinked cabin detail, © John Telford Photography.

Page viii: Sunstone detail, © Lee Groberg.

Page ix: William Weeks sketch of Nauvoo Temple, courtesy of Family and Church History Department. Photographer: Maren E. Ogden.

Page x: Early morning Nauvoo, Illinois, © John Telford Photography.

Page 1: Col. Thomas L. Kane, courtesy of Family and Church History Department.

Page 1: Nauvoo graveyard, © Don Thorpe.

Page 2: Joseph Smith's Mansion House, Nauvoo, Illinois, courtesy of Community of Christ Archives, Independence, MO.

Page 2: Pepperbox pistol carried by Joseph Smith at Carthage, © Intellectual Reserve, Inc. Courtesy of the

Museum of Church History and Art. Used by permission.

Page 3: *The Mormon Temple at Nauvoo, Ill.,* a detail of panorama engraving by J. R. Smith, 1846, *Grahams Magazine,* Vol. XXIV, April 1849, Philadelphia.

Page 4: Nauvoo Temple, courtesy of Family and Church History Department.

Page 4: Tools used to build the Nauvoo Temple, courtesy of the Museum of Church History and Art. Photographer: Maren E. Ogden.

Page 5: Nauvoo Temple with scaffolding on tower, © John Telford Photography.

Page 6: Background etching: *The Nauvoo Temple,* courtesy Illinois State Historical Library, Old State Capitol Building, Springfield, IL 62701.

Page 6: President Gordon B. Hinckley, courtesy of Family and Church History Department.

Page 7: Flag across Moroni statue on top of the Nauvoo Temple, © Lee Groberg.

Page 7: Moroni statue and American flag on crane being raised to the tower of the Nauvoo Temple, © John Telford Photography.

Page 9: Temple of Luxor © 2002 PhotoDisc, Inc.

Page 10: The Parthenon on the Acropolis in Greece, © Lee Groberg.

Page 11: Capernaum ruins detail showing star of David, © Don Thorpe.

Page 11: Capernaum ruins, © Don Thorpe.

Page 11: Sketch of star window and starstone for Nauvoo Temple by William Weeks, courtesy of Family and Church History Department. Photographer: Maren E. Ogden.

Page 11: Stone background from fragment of original Nauvoo Temple, courtesy of the Museum of Church History and Art. Photographer: Maren E. Ogden.

Page 13: *Solomon Builds the Temple,* engraving by Julius Schnorr von Carolsfeld, *Treasury of Bible Illustrations,* Dover Publications.

Page 14: *Jesus with the Doctors,* engraving by Gustave Doré, *The Doré Bible Illustrations,* Dover Publications.

Page 14: Temple of Luxor © 2002 PhotoDisc, Inc.

Page 14: Parthenon, © Lee Groberg.

Page 14: Harod's Temple model city in Jerusalem, © Floyd Holdman.

Page 15: *Joseph Smith: Prophet of the Restoration,* © Gary E. Smith.

Page 15: The Kirtland Temple, courtesy of Family and Church History Department.

Page 15: *The Nauvoo Temple,* © Intellectual Reserve, Inc. Courtesy of the Museum of Church History and Art. Used by permission.

Page 15: Nauvoo Temple under construction, © John Telford Photography.

Page 16: *The Vision,* © Intellectual Reserve, Inc. Courtesy of the Museum of Church History and Art. Used by permission.

Page 17: The All-Seeing Eye, detail of a sketch of the Nauvoo Temple by William Weeks, courtesy of Family and Church History Department. Photographer: Maren E. Ogden.

Page 18: The Kirtland Temple, courtesy of Family and Church History Department.

Page 19: *American Prophet,* © Del Parson.

Page 20: Flying angel Moroni sketch by William Weeks, courtesy of Family and Church History Department. Photographer: Maren E. Ogden.

Page 21: Moroni statue in shipping crate, © John Telford Photography.

Page 21: Moroni statue being placed on tower with a crane, © John Telford Photography.

Page 21: Detail of Karl Quilter sculpting Moroni statue, © Lee Groberg.

Page 21: Karl Quilter sculpting Moroni statue, © Lee Groberg.

Page 21: LaVar Walgren applying gold leaf to Moroni statue, © Lee Groberg.

Page 22: *Map of the City of Nauvoo,* drawn by Gustavus

Hills 1842, printed by J. Childs 1845, © Intellectual Reserve, Inc. Courtesy of the Museum of Church History and Art. Used by permission.

Page 22: Map and sketch cases, courtesy of the Museum of Church History and Art. Photographer: Maren E. Ogden.

Page 22: Background photo: *View of Nauvoo, Illinois, from Temple Site to River*, courtesy of Illinois State Historical Library, Old State Capitol Building, Springfield, IL 62701.

Page 24: Liberty Jail, courtesy of Family and Church History Department.

Page 24: Charles Scholz, © Lee Groberg.

Page 24: Nancy Naomi Alexander Tracy, courtesy of Family and Church History Department.

Page 25: *View of Quincy and the Mississippi bottom, from Col. Mays in Marion County MO,* drawn by R. B. Price, courtesy of Illinois State Historical Library, Old State Capitol Building, Springfield, IL 62701.

Page 25: Truman G. Madsen, © Lee Groberg.

Page 26: View of Nauvoo, Illinois, from river with cottage in foreground, courtesy Illinois State Historical Library, Old State Capitol Building, Springfield, IL 62701.

Page 27: Charcoal sketch of city of Nauvoo, © Gary E. Smith.

Page 28: Charcoal sketch of citizens of Nauvoo voting, © Gary E. Smith.

Page 28: Photograph of Nauvoo Temple, © Intellectual Reserve, Inc. Courtesy of the Museum of Church History and Art. Used by permission.

Page 28-29: City of Nauvoo

from Bluff Park, copyright by Frank Coulty, Nauvoo Ill. courtesy of Family and Church History Department.

Page 29: Photo of Joseph Smith cabin, Nauvoo, Illinois, © John Telford Photography.

Page 29: Josiah Quincy, courtesy of Family and Church History Department.

Page 30: President Gordon B. Hinckley, courtesy of Family and Church History Department.

Page 30-31: *Nauvoo, from the Mississippi, looking down the river,* courtesy of Illinois State Historical Library, Old State Capitol Building, Springfield, IL 62701.

Page 32: Stone-working drills, courtesy of the Museum of Church History and Art. Photographer: Maren E. Ogden.

Page 32-33: Background image: workers at the stone quarry, © Lee Groberg. Photographer: Lauri Eskelson.

Page 33: Wooden mallet and stone-working drills, courtesy of the Museum of Church History and Art. Photographer: Maren E. Ogden.

Page 33: Man in quarry working on cutting stone, © Lee Groberg. Photographer: Lauri Eskelson.

Page 34: Depiction of sickness in Nauvoo, photograph courtesy of Liz Lemon Swindle.

Page 35: Model of Nauvoo Temple, © Intellectual Reserve, Inc. Used by permission.

Page 36: *Mississippi River, Nauvoo from Montrose—Oct. 1848,* graphite drawing by Seth Eastman (1808–1875), © Intellectual Reserve, Inc. Courtesy of the Museum of

Church History and Art. Used by permission.

Page 37: Nauvoo Temple china plate, © Intellectual Reserve, Inc. Used by permission. Photographer: Welden Andersen.

Page 38: Drafting tools and sketches, courtesy of the Museum of Church History and Art. Photographer: Maren E. Ogden.

Page 39: Drafting tools, courtesy of the Museum of Church History and Art. Photographer: Maren E. Ogden.

Page 39: Entablature sketch by William Weeks, courtesy of Family and Church History Department. Photographer; Maren E. Ogden.

Page 40: All photos: glass-making, glazing, and east window, © Lee Groberg.

Page 41: Detail of engraving *The Nauvoo Temple,* courtesy Illinois State Historical Library, Old State Capitol Building, Springfield, IL 62701.

Page 41: Detail of sketch by William Weeks of the Nauvoo Temple, courtesy of Family and Church History Department. Photographer: Maren E. Ogden.

Page 41: Glen Leonard, courtesy of the Museum of Church History and Art.

Page 42: William Allred, courtesy of Family and Church History Department.

Page 42: Depiction of hauling stone from quarry, © Lee Groberg. Photographer: Lauri Eskelson.

Page 43: Charcoal sketch of lumber raft coming down the Mississippi River to Nauvoo, Illinois, © Gary E. Smith.

Page 43: Mississippi River, © John Telford Photography.

Page 43: Charcoal sketch of men steering a lumber raft, © Gary E. Smith.

Page 44: Morning's first light shining on southeast cornerstone, © Intellectual Reserve, Inc. Used by permission. Photographer: Welden Andersen.

Page 45: Charcoal sketch of foundation of Nauvoo Temple, © Gary E. Smith.

Page 45: President Hinckley putting first mortar on cornerstone, © Lee Groberg.

Page 46: Norton Jacobs, courtesy of Family and Church History Department.

Page 46: Wandle Mace, courtesy of Family and Church History Department.

Page 47: *Nauvoo Legion Benevolent Association banner,* painting by Danquart A. Weggeland, © Intellectual Reserve, Inc. Courtesy of the Museum of Church History and Art. Used by permission.

Page 47: *Joseph Mustering the Nauvoo Legion,* by C. C. A. Christensen, © Brigham Young University Museum of Art. All rights reserved.

Page 47: Joseph Smith pistol—Nauvoo, © Intellectual Reserve, Inc. Courtesy of the Museum of Church History and Art. Used by permission.

Page 48: Wooden caddy for tithing donations and tithing record, courtesy of the Museum of Church History and Art. Photographer: Maren E. Ogden.

Page 49: Basket and apple © PhotoDisc, Inc.

Page 49: Zina Diantha Huntington, courtesy Family and Church History Dept.

Page 49: Detail of tithing donation record, courtesy Museum of Church History and Art. Photographer: Maren E. Ogden.

Page 50: Wagon on raft © John Telford Photography.

Page 50-51: Background leather © PhotoDisc, Inc.

Page 52: *Hurrah, Hurrah for Israel,* © Robert T. Barrett.

Page 52: *Millennial Star,* courtesy of Family and Church History Department.

Page 53: John Butler, © Lee Groberg.

Page 53: Brigham Young, courtesy of Family and Church History Department.

Page 54-55: Gathering in Nauvoo map by Paul Jager.

Page 56-57: *Embarkation of the Saints from Liverpool,* by Ken Baxter, © Intellectual Reserve, Inc. Courtesy of the Museum of Church History and Art. Used by permission.

Page 57: William Clayton, courtesy of Family and Church History Department.

Page 58: St. James Chapel, Staffordshire, England, © Lee Groberg.

Page 58: Stone bridge in England, © Lee Groberg.

Page 59: Nauvoo Temple daguerreotype by Louis Rice Chaffin, courtesy of Family and Church History Department.

Page 60: Charles Lambert, courtesy of Family and Church History Department.

Page 60: Bronze statue of Joseph and Hyrum Smith, © Intellectual Reserve, Inc. Used by permission. Photographer: Welden Andersen.

Page 61: Sketch showing spiral staircase by William Weeks, courtesy of Family and Church History Department. Photographer: Maren E. Ogden.

Page 61: Stone fragments from original Nauvoo Temple, courtesy of Museum of Church History and Art. Photographer: Maren E. Ogden.

Page 61: Detail of starstone from a sketch by William

Weeks, courtesy of Family and Church History Department. Photographer: Maren E. Ogden.

Page 61: Background: Detail of stone fragment from original Nauvoo Temple, courtesy of Museum of Church History and Art. Photographer: Maren E. Ogden.

Page 62: *Organization of the Relief Society, 17 March 1842,* by Dale Kilbourn, © Intellectual Reserve, Inc. Used by permission.

Page 64: Rodney Davis, © Lee Groberg.

Page 64-65: *The Nauvoo Temple,* by C. C. A. Christensen (image is cropped), © Brigham Young University Museum of Art. All rights reserved.

Page 66-67: Background: Quarry reenactment, by Lauri Eskelson, © Lee Groberg.

Page 67: Starstone detail, © Lee Groberg.

Page 67: Sunstone face, courtesy of Museum of Church History and Art. Photographer: Maren E. Ogden.

Page 67: Moonstone detail, © John Telford Photography.

Page 68: Round wooden mallet, courtesy of Museum of Church History and Art. Photographer: Maren E. Ogden.

Page 68-69: Quarry reenactment of stonemason working on sunstone face, by Lauri Eskelson, © Lee Groberg.

Page 70-71: Background: Detail of stone fragment from original Nauvoo Temple, courtesy of Museum

of Church History and Art. Photographer: Maren E. Ogden.

Page 70-71: Detail of starstones and star windows from sketch by William Weeks, courtesy of Family and Church History Department. Photographer: Maren E. Ogden.

Page 70: Richard Ahlborn, © Lee Groberg.

Page 70-71: Sunstones in a row, © Lee Groberg.

Page 71: Detail of shims between the two pieces of a sunstone, courtesy of Museum of Church History and Art. Photographer: Maren E. Ogden.

Page 71: Detail of starstone, © Lee Groberg.

Page 71: Lucien Batalu working on moonstone, © Lee Groberg.

Page 71: Virgil Badic working on sunstone, © Lee Groberg.

Page 72: Stone crew in front of first moonstone placed on Nauvoo Temple, © Lee Groberg.

Page 72: Sunstone being raised on a crane to place on Nauvoo Temple, © Lee Groberg.

Page 72: Row of sunstone pilasters, © Lee Groberg.

Page 74: Mississippi River, © John Telford Photography.

Page 75: Charcoal sketch of baptisms in Mississippi River, Nauvoo, © Gary E. Smith.

Page 75: John Lundquist, © Lee Groberg.

Page 76: Wilford Woodruff, courtesy of Family and Church History Department.

Page 76: Charcoal sketch of oxen on baptismal font, © Gary E. Smith.

Page 76-77: Placing oxen for baptismal font, © Lee Groberg.

Page 76: Wade Udall carving one of the oxen, © Lee Groberg.

Page 76: Fragment of the nose of original ox in baptistry, courtesy of Museum of Church History and Art. Photographer: Maren E. Ogden.

Page 77: Charcoal sketch of Elijah Fordham carving original ox from pine planks, © Gary E. Smith.

Page 77: Original drain from under the font, courtesy of Museum of Church History and Art. Photographer: Maren E. Ogden.

Page 77: Bricks from the floor of the original baptistry, courtesy of Museum of Church History and Art. Photographer: Maren E. Ogden.

Page 79: *Joseph Smith,* © William Whitaker, oil on canvas.

Page 79: Red Brick Store, Nauvoo, Illinois, courtesy of Family and Church History Department.

Page 81: Sunstone, © Lee Groberg.

Page 82: Parley P. Pratt, courtesy of Family and Church History Department.

Page 82: First Presidency inspecting a sunstone, © Lee Groberg.

Page 83: *The Nauvoo Temple,* courtesy Illinois State Historical Library, Old State Capitol Building, Springfield, IL 62701.

Page 84: *The Battle of Nauvoo,* by C. C. A. Christensen, © Brigham Young University Museum of Art. All rights reserved.

Page 84-85: Background: Charcoal sketch of settlement outside Nauvoo being attacked by mob, © Gary E. Smith.

Page 86-87: Scenic of Nauvoo, artist unknown, © Intellectual Reserve, Inc. Used by permission.

Page 89: *Joseph Smith Directing the Nauvoo Legion,* 1887, oil on canvas, by John Hafen © Intellectual Reserve, Inc. Courtesy of Museum of Church History and Art. Used by permission.

Page 89: Nauvoo Legion sword and scabbard which belonged to Jonathan H. Hale, © Intellectual Reserve, Inc. Courtesy of Museum of Church History and Art. Used by permission.

Page 90: Charles Foster, courtesy of Family and Church History Department.

Page 90: Eliza R. Snow, courtesy of Family and Church History Department.

Page 90-91: Last page of the Nauvoo Charter, courtesy of Family and Church History Department.

Page 91: First page of the Nauvoo Charter, courtesy of Family and Church History Department.

Page 91: Certified statement from Nauvoo Charter, courtesy of Family and Church History Department.

Page 92: Typeset trays in Grandin Building, Palmyra, New York, © Douglas L. Powell.

Page 92: Press in Grandin Building, Palmyra, New York, © Paul E. Gilbert.

Page 92-93: *Nauvoo Expositor,* courtesy of Family and Church History Department.

Page 93: John Taylor, courtesy of Family and Church History Department.

Page 94: "The Old Jail at Carthage, where Joseph Smith the Mormon Prophet was killed," courtesy Illinois State Historical Library, Old

State Capitol Building, Springfield, IL 62701.

Page 95: *Exterior of Carthage Jail,* by C. C. A. Christensen (image is cropped), © Brigham Young University Museum of Art. All rights reserved.

Page 96: *Portrait of Joseph Smith,* by Danquardt A. Weggeland, © Intellectual Reserve, Inc. Courtesy of Museum of Church History and Art. Used by permission.

Page 97: Mary Alice Cannon Lambert, courtesy of Family and Church History Department.

Page 97: Vilate Kimball, courtesy of Family and Church History Department.

Page 97: *Times and Seasons,* courtesy of Family and Church History Department.

Page 98-99: *Nauvoo, Illinois,* mid-1840 © Dan Thornton. For prints go to www.villagepiazza.com.

Page 100: Charcoal sketch of capstone being placed on Nauvoo Temple, © Gary E. Smith.

Page 101: William W. Phelps, courtesy of Family and Church History Department.

Page 101: Brigham Young, courtesy of Family and Church History Department.

Page 102: Stonemason working on sunstone from quarry reenactment, by Lauri Eskelson, © Lee Groberg.

Page 102: Detail of texture in stone fragment from original Nauvoo Temple, courtesy of Museum of Church History and Art. Photographer: Maren E. Ogden.

Page 103: Governor Thomas Ford, courtesy of Family and Church History Department.

Page 104: *Nauvoo the Beautiful,* © Larry C. Winborg.

Page 105: William Clayton, courtesy of Family and Church History Department.

Page 106: Helen Mar Whitney, courtesy of Family and Church History Department.

Page 106-107: Charcoal sketch of capstone being placed on Nauvoo Temple, © Gary E. Smith.

Page 108: George A. Smith, courtesy of Family and Church History Department.

Page 108: Loren N. Horton, © Lee Groberg.

Page 109: Charcoal sketch of settlement outside of Nauvoo being attacked by a mob, © Gary E. Smith.

Page 110: Stacey A. Dickerson adjusting the hands of the clock, © Lee Groberg.

Page 110: Detail of the tower from a sketch by William Weeks, courtesy of Museum of Church History and Art. Photographer: Maren E. Ogden.

Page 110: Temple bell, © John Telford Photography.

Page 110: Detail of dates on temple bell, © John Telford Photography.

Page 112: *View from Temple Hill,* © Gary E. Smith.

Page 113: Warren Foote, courtesy of Family and Church History Department.

Page 113: Edwin S. Gaustad, © Lee Groberg.

Page 114: *Crossing the Mississippi on the Ice,* by C. C. A. Christensen, © Brigham Young University Museum of Art. All rights reserved.

Page 116-117: Charcoal sketch of the Saints building wagons to move west, © Gary E. Smith.

Page 118: *The Mormon Temple - Der Mormonentempel,* H. Lewis pinx, Lith. Jnst. Arnz & Co. Dusseldorf. Courtesy Illinois State Historical Library, Old State Capitol Building, Springfield, IL 62701.

Page 121: *The Temple at Nauvoo,* engraving, believed to have been produced by an individual surnamed Vizetelly in the late 1840s–50s, courtesy of Family and Church History Department.

Page 122: Erastus Snow, courtesy of Family and Church History Department.

Page 122: Jacob Neusner, © Lee Groberg.

Page 123: Quincy Rifleman minutes, © Lee Groberg.

Page 124: *Mormons in Wagons at Nauvoo,* engraving. Image has been tinted, and a color background inserted behind it. Used by permission, State Historical Society of Missouri, Columbia.

Page 125: Box of tools used on the Nauvoo Temple, courtesy of Museum of Church History and Art. Photographer: Maren E. Ogden.

Page 126: Detail of bronze relief in Nauvoo, Illinois, © John Telford Photography.

Page 127: Samuel Richards, courtesy of Family and Church History Department.

Page 128-129: Keys from the Nauvoo Temple, © Lee Groberg.

Page 130: *Burning of the Temple,* by C. C. A. Christensen, © Brigham Young University Museum of Art. All rights reserved.

Page 131: Burning of the temple reenactment, © John Telford Photography.

Page 132-133: *Ruins of the Nauvoo Temple,* engraving by C. Fenn from drawing by Frederick Hawkins Piercy, 1853, © Intellectual Reserve, Inc. Courtesy of Museum of Church History and Art. Used by permission.

Page 133: *Nauvoo on the Mississippi,* by unknown artist, ca. 1850, © Intellectual Reserve, Inc. Courtesy of Museum of Church History and Art. Used by permission.

Page 134-135: *The Beautiful: A Gift to Joseph* © Al Rounds.

Page 136: James Clarke—Iowa Territorial Governor, courtesy of Special Collections, State Historical Society of Iowa - Des Moines.

Page 137: *City of Joseph,* © Eric Dowdle. For print information visit www.dowdle-folkart.com.

Page 138: Carol Meyers, © Lee Groberg.

Page 139: Sunset through window of the Nauvoo Temple, © Lee Groberg.

Page 140: Crowd at groundbreaking ceremony for Nauvoo Temple, © Darrel Chamberlain Photography.

Page 140: Construction of Nauvoo Temple showing foundation © Lee Groberg.

Page 140: Construction of Nauvoo Temple showing concrete walls several stories high © Lee Groberg.

Page 140: Construction of Nauvoo Temple showing interior scaffolding © Lee Groberg.

Page 141: Construction of Nauvoo Temple showing exterior ready for finish stone © Lee Groberg.

Page 141: Construction of Nauvoo Temple showing limestone veneer placed on exterior © Lee Groberg.

Page 141: Construction of Nauvoo Temple showing scaffolding on tower © Lee Groberg.

Page 141: Construction of Nauvoo Temple showing starstones being placed © Lee Groberg.

Page 142: Colored glass star window © Lee Groberg.

Page 142: Detail of work being done on skylight © Lee Groberg.

Page 142: Tom Holdman sketching baptismal art glass panel © Lee Groberg.

Page 142: Tom Holdman working on baptismal art glass panel © Lee Groberg.

Page 143: Bench in Nauvoo Temple © Intellectual Reserve, Inc. Used by permission. Photographer: Welden Andersen.

Page 144: Sketches of the Nauvoo Temple by William Weeks, courtesy of Family and Church History Department. Photographer: Maren E. Ogden.

Page 144-145: Detail of Assembly Hall in Nauvoo Temple, © Intellectual Reserve, Inc. Used by permission. Photographer: Welden Andersen.

Page 145: Sketch of the exterior of the Nauvoo Temple by William Weeks, courtesy of Family and Church History Department. Photographer: Maren E. Ogden.

Page 146: Stone fragment from original Nauvoo Temple, courtesy of the Museum of Church History and Art. Photographer: Maren E. Ogden.

Page 146: Basketweave pattern in stone © Lee Groberg.

Page 146: Background: vertical striation detail from original Nauvoo Temple, cour-tesy of the Museum of Church History and Art. Photographer: Maren E. Ogden.

Page 147: Spiral staircase in Nauvoo Temple © Intellectual Reserve, Inc. Used by permission. Photographer: Welden Andersen.

Page 148-149: Celestial room skylight in Nauvoo Temple, © Intellectual Reserve, Inc. Used by permission. Photographer: Welden Andersen.

Page 150: Doug Fryer working on mural for Nauvoo Temple © Lee Groberg.

Page 150: Hanging a mural in the Nauvoo Temple © Lee Groberg.

Page 150: Gary E. Smith touching up a corner of a mural in the Nauvoo Temple © Lee Groberg.

Page 150-151: Robert Marshall painting a mural for the Nauvoo Temple © Lee Groberg.

Page 151: Group photo of all the artists painting murals for the Nauvoo Temple © Lee Groberg.

Page 151: Frank Magleby painting a mural for the Nauvoo Temple © Lee Groberg.

Page 151: Chris Young and James Christensen discussing final touches on murals in the Nauvoo Temple © Lee Groberg.

Page 151: James Christensen painting a mural for the Nauvoo Temple © Lee Groberg.

Page 152: Baptismal font under construction © John Telford Photography.

Page 152: Assembly Hall in Nauvoo Temple, © Intellectual Reserve, Inc. Used by permission. Photographer: Welden Andersen.

Page 153: Celestial Room in Nauvoo Temple, © Intellectual Reserve, Inc. Used by permission. Photographer: Welden Andersen.

Page 155: Detail of door frame in World Room in Nauvoo Temple, © Intellectual Reserve, Inc. Used by permission. Photographer: Welden Andersen.

Page 156: Nauvoo Temple on 156th anniversary of Exodus from Nauvoo, © 2002 Fly Guy Photos, Arlo Sinele.

Back Endsheet: Daguerreotype of the Nauvoo Temple (drawn on weather vane), ca. 1845, unknown photographer, courtesy of Family and Church History Department.